15 STEPS TO SPIRITUAL HEALING

MAKING PEACE
with
Yourself

By Kathryn James Hermes, FSP

With poetry by Bernadette M. Reis, FSP

auline
BOOKS & MEDIA
Boston

Library of Congress Cataloging-in-Publication Data

Hermes, Kathryn.
  Making peace with yourself : 15 steps to spiritual healing /
by Kathryn James Hermes.
      p. cm.
  Includes bibliographical references.
  ISBN 0-8198-4859-X
  1. Peace of mind—Religious aspects—Christianity. 2. Spirituality.
I. Title.
  BV4908.5.H47 2007
  248.4'82—dc22

                                        2007007675

Cover design by Rosana Usselmann

Cover photo by Mary Emmanuel Alves, FSP

"P" and PAULINE are registered trademarks of the Daughters of St. Paul.

Published by Pauline Books & Media, 50 Saint Paul's Avenue, Boston, MA 02130-3491. www.pauline.org.

Printed in the U.S.A.

Pauline Books & Media is the publishing house of the Daughters of St. Paul, an international congregation of women religious serving the Church with the communications media.

1 2 3 4 5 6 7 8 9   12 11 10 09 08 07

To those who have shared
their lives with me...
Courage.

∼

To all who seek inner peace...
Believe.

∼

To all who have added their expertise
to these pages...
Thanks.

Contents

∽ PART ONE: LOVE ∽

∼ PART TWO: HEALING ∼

∼ PART THREE: MYSTERY ∼

The Promise

THIS BOOK IS A FORAY into the reality of life—exactly as we experience it. No one would deny that life is a precious gift, but reality also teaches us that it includes its share of pain, suffering, and the cross. Life cannot be controlled or manipulated or rearranged according to our own agenda. Life just is, and we must learn to make peace with ourselves and with our lives just as they are. Sometimes our immediate reactions to the painful events of life are to sue, to rage, to lash out. But is there something deeper than the litigations rife in society today, deeper than the disappointments and injustices so many suffer? What explains the unfairness of life, and how do we live with this unfairness?

The lives and writings of holy people, past and present, and the wealth of the Scriptures open up to us a different way of accepting life's realities. They point out a path toward making peace with ourselves. That way is complete and utter self-abandonment to God, until we *see* the deepest reality at work in the world and in our lives. As we begin to live in that reality, everything else falls into place. Life does not become easy. We aren't spared disaster. However, we can give ourselves to life with complete assurance that God always has our best interests at heart.

Acknowledgments

ALL OF THE STORIES contained in these pages have been shared with me throughout the past years. Names and identifying details have often been changed to protect people's privacy. In some cases I have used composites of stories.

Kind permission had been granted for the use of the following extracts:

Gregory of Nyssa: The Life of Moses, by Abraham J. Malherbe and Everett Ferguson, copyright © 1978 by Paulist Press, Inc., New York/Mahwah, NJ. Used with permission. www.paulistpress.com.

Women's Spirituality: Resources for Development, edited by Joann Wolski Coinn, copyright © 1996 by Paulist Press, Inc., New York/Mahwah, N.J. Used with permission. www.paulistpress.com.

The Wellspring of Worship, by Jean Corbon, copyright © 2005 by Ignatius Press, San Francisco. Used with permission.

Confession, by Jean Corbon, copyright © 1985 by Ignatius Press, San Francisco. Used with permission.

The Victory of Love, by Adrienne von Speyr, copyright © 1990 by Ignatius Press, San Francisco. Used with permission.

Light Over the Scaffold, by Augustin-Michel Lemonnier, copyright © 1996 by Alba House, New York. Used with permission.

Thoughts of Saint Therese the Little Flower of Jesus, by Therese of Lisieux, copyright © 1915 by P. J. Kenedy & Sons, New York. Used with permission.

I Believe in Love, by Jean du Coeur de Jésus d'Elbée, published by Sophia Institute Press in 2001. Used with permission.

Theology of the Eucharistic Table, by Jeremy Driscoll, OSB, copyright © 2003 by Gracewing Publishing. Used with permission.

Renovare Spiritual Formation Bible, by Renovare and edited by Richard J. Foster, copyright © 2005 by Renovare, Inc.

Published by HarperCollins, New York. Used with permission.

St. John Vianney, as quoted by Alfred Monnin, *The Curé of Ars*, (St. Louis: Herder, 1927). Used with permission.

Living with Sickness: A Struggle Toward Meaning, copyright © Susan Saint Sing, Ph.D., published in 1987 by St. Anthony Messenger Press, Cincinnati. Used with permission.

From Glory to Glory, by Jean Danielou, copyright © 1961 by Scribner. Used with permission.

Self-Abandonment to Divine Providence, by Jean-Pierre De Caussade, copyright © 1959 by Burns, Oates and Washbourne, Ltd. Used with permission.

Search for Nothing: The Life of John of the Cross, by Richard P. Hardy, copyright © 1982 by Crossroad Publishing Company, New York. Used with permission.

Maria Was His Middle Name: Day by Day with Bl. Maximilian Kolbe, copyright © 1977 by Benziger Sisters Publishers. Used with permission.

Introduction

EVERY ONCE IN A WHILE, when God really wants to get through to me, I catch a bad cold, lose my voice, and have to spend a couple of days alone. The last time this happened, I woke up one morning with a severe sore throat and the beginnings of laryngitis. Since I had a radio interview over the phone that evening, I nursed my sore throat with every "home remedy" the sisters of my community suggested to me. I gargled with various combinations of hot and cold water, vinegar, salt, and crushed aspirin. I drank what seemed like gallons of warm water and honey with lemon juice, and kept silent most of the day in order to save my voice. By five that evening I felt much better, and, hanging over a vaporizer, I went through with the interview. The next morning I woke up without a voice. Thus began my solitary sojourn.

I retired to my room with my computer and several writing projects, a few letters to answer, and a couple of books I had wanted to read. As I tried to settle myself in for this stretch of solitude, I felt anxious and noted my inner resistance. I lit a candle next to Rublev's icon of the Trinity and began to pray psalms from the Liturgy of the Hours. "O God, you are my God, for whom I long.... With all my heart I praise you.... You are the desire of my soul...." Rather than calming me, the words swept through my mind like a brisk wind.

I wandered through the pages of various books, unable to brush off a peculiar restlessness. Finally, I just stopped and gazed at the icon. Though the silence was thick around me, it was somehow comforting, like a warm blanket after coming in from a cold November day. With voices and deadlines and ideas settling to the back of my mind, I slowly began to befriend the silence. After some time I found myself simply listening to the absence of noise and enjoying it. The silence divided me from my ordinary life, providing distance and relief. The more I sat, simply satisfied with being present to God, the more I realized that my anxiousness was only an indication of a much deeper inner restlessness. Instead of a mosaic of feelings, events, ideals, and desires, my identity had become more like a box of puzzle pieces scraped together from several different puzzles, none of them fitting together or making sense. I seemed to hear with relief, "It's time to come to your heart."

Inside each of us, deep in our hearts, is a place of peace and rest. We cannot reach this place by plane or car but only through stillness. Today's society is full of people who, just like you and I, long to make peace with themselves. They find themselves in all sorts of circumstances: unexpected illnesses, financial struggles, employment issues, relationship difficulties, situations of injustice, brushes with the law, experiences of personal vulnerability and failure, bouts of boredom, and grapplings with faith. These situations are complex and unpredictable. In mysterious ways they cause people to plumb the depths of the spirit, searching for peace—or at least relief. Sometimes these situations may seem unredeemable.

In 2004, when over 150,000 people died in the tsunami, many asked, "Where was God? Why didn't he stop this from happening?" Someone I met on an Internet forum discussing this tragic event wrote:

> I totally lost my faith forty years ago, when I was up close and personal with a disaster of similar magnitude. I was an electronics technician in the U.S. Navy, stationed on a ship outside Hong Kong. My job was to keep communications open with the planes that were "watching" over Indochina. It was in the early 1960s, during Mao's Great Leap Forward. Millions of people were starving in China, and the stream of refugees into the British Crown Colony of Hong Kong was phenomenal.
>
> On top of the horrid conditions, which left thousands dead every day, a typhoon bore directly down upon this area. I had been stationed on a flotilla in the harbor when the storm hit. After days of "cleanup," we were finally ordered back to the ship. As I stepped over one last blind little boy, he raised his arms to me for help. I broke out in a run.
>
> On ship I grabbed a bottle of gin to wash from my memory what I had seen. Then I went to the chapel and cried for hours. The chaplain asked me what was wrong. I said to him, "Except for the accident of time and place, that little boy could have been my baby brother!" The chaplain shook his head and said that these people were Communists and were only getting what they deserved. I left the chapel, determined *never* to darken the doors of a church again!

Although tragedy and malicious words had propelled this man, David, into an almost forty-year hiatus from God and the Church, somehow he eventually found inner peace and could then reach out to others who had the same questions he had struggled with. "It took me a long time to come back to the Church," David wrote, "and I was on and off for too many years. It was when I finally came to terms with the fact that we have to base our Faith on *faith* that things changed dramatically."

A WOMAN IN THE EARLY 1800s set sail from New York to Italy in a desperate attempt to save her husband's life. Once a woman of great wealth, she had sold her last possessions to pay for the trip, leaving all but one of her children behind in New York in the care of others. When she and her husband and child arrived in a seaport of Italy, they were quarantined in a nearby stone tower because of a yellow fever epidemic that had been raging when they left New York City. The Felicchi family, friends of theirs in Italy, sent food to them as often as possible. But the cold, damp tower sapped away her husband's remaining health. Two days after their release, he died, leaving the woman and her children penniless and alone.

Today we might sue those responsible for the conditions of that confinement. Instead, this young widow repeated words she had written two years earlier, that her soul was "sensibly convinced of an entire surrender of itself and all its faculties to God." Elizabeth Ann Seton had found peace.

ARE THE INDIVIDUALS in these two stories crazy or naïve? Where did they get their certainty of God's goodness? How could they place the puzzle pieces of their lives into the hands of God and expect him to hold them together? Did they know something that many of us have forgotten or perhaps never learned? Each of us passes through puzzling days, months, or even years in life. They may not be as dramatic as imprisonment or the death of a loved one. They can be as amazingly simple as being out of touch with our own hearts, the result of overwork or overstress.

This book will explore the stories of people like you and me, people who faced situations that often seemed unredeemable, people who needed to make peace with themselves. In these pages we will explore the puzzles of *their* lives so that we can piece together the puzzles of our own.

Meeting God in the Silence

My bouts of restlessness are frequent, abated only through serious attention to listening and contemplation. As endless nervous memories and worries tug at my consciousness, I find God and rediscover his reliability only if I regularly abandon myself into his hands in silence.

This book can help you attain the "heart of silence" through the stillness of contemplation. Each chapter presents a step toward peace, for only in being still can we discover that God *is*. You are invited to pray with these steps not just once, but many times. They are meant to lead you progressively deeper into the stillness in which you can make peace with yourself. You are invited to pray your way through this book, working your way gently through each of the exercises.

Each step includes a story of an ordinary person who searched for and found peace. Our imaginations need to "see" and "hear" and "taste" God's presence and activity in people like ourselves. Once we become attuned to God's workings in others, we can more easily discover him at work in our own lives. Each step also explores the Scriptures to uncover the face of the God, who alone gives us the gift of inner peace. The chapters move through the books of the Bible, from Genesis to the Book of Revelation.

Since the Incarnation, the human and the divine are so closely intertwined that Christian spirituality has protected the integrity of each and the communion of both. By coming to terms with our own histories, personalities, circumstances, wounds, and realities, we become able to make our peace with God.

How to Use This Book

Contemplative prayer doesn't necessarily mean solitary prayer. You may want to do at least some of the steps with a friend or spiritual companion or guide. As Christians, even as we pray alone, we are part of a communion of believers brought together in Christ. Since the days of the Desert Fathers and Mothers, Christianity has acknowledged and availed itself of the wisdom of companionship on the spiritual journey.

You will need very few things for these prayer steps: a quiet space conducive to prayer, a Bible, a notebook to jot down thoughts and feelings, a pen, and a highlighter.

These chapters, both in their themes and in the focus of their guided prayer, progressively build on one another. Though you may be tempted to jump into the first chapter that grabs your attention, remember that the purpose of the book is not to give you answers. The book is meant to lead you to peace with yourself, and it will do so if you follow its gentle guidance down the winding paths of your life. You may even find yourself lingering with one of the steps, using the prayer guide again and again. Or while you are working your way through this book, a situation in your life may lead you to return to an earlier step. Follow these inspirations.

If at any time you find the feelings associated with exploring these issues to be overwhelming, I encourage you to contact a spiritual director or counselor and discuss with him or her what is going on in your mind and heart. Though you may share this journey with a spiritual director, a friend, or a prayer group, remember most of all to share it with God.

PART ONE

Love

September Psalm

Calm my restless spirit, my terrified soul.
Lead me to that haven where I may behold
your beauty, peace, and joy hid behind the vale of tears.

Restore my peace of mind, heal my fearful heart.
Take me to that lonely, quiet place apart.
There my soul will find rest in the shadows of the night.

Revive my drooping spirit, my downcast will.
Pour your soothing oil over my wounds until
death has lost its hold on me and new life enters in.

Then will my soul rejoice—my spirit sing praise.
To you will I make music throughout my days.
For now you are Comforter, Healer, Savior, Father.

Settling Down

MAKING PEACE WITH ONESELF begins with awareness—becoming aware of who you are and aware of who God is, responsive to the subtle communication that is going on between you. That takes a lot of work on our part, at least initially: to settle down, loosen, let go, forget, turn off the endless mental activity and emotional responses so that we can encounter what is truly real about God and about ourselves.

Begin by becoming aware of the exterior world around you.

> Listen for a few moments.
> What do you hear?
> Now let these things go.
> Let them slide into oblivion.
> Let them go.
> The dogs will continue to bark, the refrigerator hum.
> Cars honk, radios blare.
> They do not need to hook your attention.
> Let them slide by.
> Enjoy the new sense of peace.

Now begin to interrupt the endless mental chattering, quieting the thoughts and emotions that kidnap the consciousness. As you quiet down, begin to pull apart the mass of "thoughts and emotions" by simply saying the word "thinking" softly to yourself as you become aware of your thoughts.

When you are aware of these individual thoughts and reactions, you can begin to let them go.

Picture before you a stone wall, endlessly high and endlessly long.

The wall is directly in front of you, only a few inches from your face.

You can see nothing else but this wall.

Let your attention rest on the wall for several minutes, an exercise that helps your thoughts drop away.

Imagine yourself to be like a stone.

Feel yourself heavy, still, and silent as a stone statue.

Let go of past events, friendships, worries, conflicts.

Let them go.

Let go of ideals, ambitions, plans, and dreams.

Let go of anything around you.

Let go of everything outside of this moment.

Let go of everything outside of this place.

Let go of everyone.

Mentally scan your body and gently tell it to relax.

Relax your shoulders, your arms, your legs, your ankles, and your feet.

Relax your forehead, your cheeks, your eyes, your jaw, and your ears.

As you do this exercise regularly, you will become more sensitive to the silence.

You will enjoy resting in the stillness.

You will begin to hear.

Listen for your own cry.

Listen for the cry of God for you.

This is an excellent preparation with which to begin every time of stillness and communion with God.

Gathering Stars

Barbara walked slowly into a church in New York City. The hectic rush of traffic receded as the immense doors closed behind her. Cautiously she stepped into the last pew, her eyes straining to see through the darkness. A tiny light at the front of the church indicated the presence of Jesus in the tabernacle. "Where were you?" she asked weakly, her eyes filling with tears as she collapsed on the pew. "Where were you when I needed you in the hospital? Where were you when my brother died? You left me all alone."

Her accusations, hurled into the darkness, almost frightened her. But nothing happened, so Barbara continued. "In fact, where were you four years ago when my oldest brother died, and two years later when my sister died?" There. It was said. God had been notified of exactly how she felt. Broken. Alone. Rejected.

Later that evening at home, the phone rang. Barbara picked it up, her voice full of the grief and exhaustion of one who had seen her siblings struggle with death and lose. "How are you doing, Barbara?" It was Sr. Mary, a lovely seventy-eight-year-old nun from whom she had often sought wisdom and comfort.

Barbara answered with an absent, "Okay." The words *Just leave me alone!* were implied, but she was too exhausted to voice them.

"I just heard a song on the radio and it brought you to mind," Sister continued in an understanding voice. "It's the song 'You Belong to My Heart.' The words made me think of you and God: 'We were gathering stars while a million guitars played our love song.'" Then she started humming the chorus in a thin voice that, for all its age, still had a little lilt:

> *Do you remember,*
> *Darling, you are the one,*
> *And you'll always belong to my heart.*[1]

"God wants you to gather stars with him, Barbara. I know you are sad now, but this will pass. You can go with God and hear his love song again and be happy once more."

Barbara quietly thanked her and ended the phone call. *Gather stars, sure,* she thought, *as if I didn't have anything else to do.* But after a while, Barbara thought about Sister's suggestion and finally decided to give it a try. She tells me it's how she now prays.

> I go gather stars with God. We sing the song together and spend time with each other. And I feel my brothers and sister present.
>
> I was speaking to a friend on the phone whose mother had died and whose daughter has cancer. I was telling her about what Sister had said to me. "Go find a song," I told my friend. "Not 'You Belong to My Heart,' because that is my song. God and I gather stars. But find another song, maybe about dancing. And dance with God. Whenever things get too hard to bear, go dance with God. God would love to dance with you."
>
> When we finished our conversation, I turned on my television and flipped to the "Easy Listening" channel. To my amazement, "You Belong to My Heart" was playing! I speed-dialed my friend and we listened to it together. We were now three on the phone: my friend, I, and God. I have

never heard the song on that channel since. So that's how I pray now. God and I gather stars, and my friend dances.

~

OFTEN, WHEN LIFE'S EVENTS break our hearts, we are ashamed of our anger and pain. We apologize for angry words and stifle cries of pain, pushing our hurts out of sight. We try to make peace with ourselves without acknowledging our anger and our tears—somehow these seem unacceptable to us. But they aren't unacceptable to God.

From the very beginning of Sacred Scripture, we find God responding to the cries of his people. In the first pages of Genesis, Cain kills Abel—two brothers, the sons of the first man and woman. In response, God calls out to Cain: "Where is your brother Abel?...What have you done? Listen; *your brother's blood is crying out to me* from the ground!" (Gen 4:9–10; emphasis added here and throughout this book).

Later, God hears the cries of the boy Joseph, who was thrown into a well by his brothers and then sold to the Ishmaelites. "The Lord was *with Joseph*" (Gen 39:2).

To Moses, God declares of the Israelites enslaved in Egypt, "I have observed the misery of my people who are in Egypt; I have *heard their cry* on account of their taskmasters. Indeed, I know their sufferings, and I have come down to deliver them" (Ex 3:7–8).

When the Israelites later stand at the Red Sea, with the Egyptians coming up fast behind them, they *cry out to the Lord*. Then they say to Moses, who has led them out of captivity, "Was it because there were no graves in Egypt that you have taken us away to die in the wilderness? What have you done to us, bringing us out of Egypt? Is this not the very thing we told you in Egypt, 'Let us alone and let us serve the Egyptians?' For it would have been better for us to serve the Egyptians than to die in the wilderness." But Moses answers the people, *"Do not be afraid, stand firm, and see the deliverance that the Lord will accomplish for you today.... The* Lord will fight for you, and you have only to keep still" (Ex 14:11–14).

God listens, hears, and delivers his people. God is moved when he hears our cries. But Scripture tells us something more. Not only is God moved, God also *does* something. God saves. God liberates. God frees. God consoles. God acts with power in our best interests.

You would think that their miraculous deliverance from the Egyptians, the greatest power on earth, would have erased any doubts the Israelites might have had about God's ability to lead them to freedom. And yet two chapters after the exodus event, the Israelites complain about the "provisions" God has given them for their journey. They angrily ask Moses to let them return to Egypt. God had listened to them. But had they listened to God?

Crying goes both ways.

Barbara let herself cry out to God, and she heard his answer in the kind, wavering voice of an elderly nun. *Gather stars with God.* Find new ways to pray, to relate to God. Let these sorrows open up in the darkened sky an immense horizon punctuated with beautiful radiance. Though Barbara wanted her siblings back with her on this earth, she found them in a new way as she found God in a new way.

Be Still

∼ *Wisdom to guide you:* "Alone we stare into black holes of space, pained and dying in our isolation. But in the decision to turn around and face the universe as it encompasses us—where we are, in our daily condition—we find countless other stars, in all directions of the darkness, twinkling."

Susan Saint Sing[2]

∼ *Scripture to hold you:* "I will turn their mourning into joy" (Jer 31:13).

∼ *Thought to sustain you:* I can find you, Lord, in a new way.

STEP TWO

Accepting the Past

TO MAKE PEACE with ourselves, we need to accept our own history. All of us have something in our past that is a source of resentment or suffering: where we were born, the school we went to, a parent's inattention. Some of us, however, have been seriously hurt by neglect, loneliness, or abuse. The process of becoming still may be too frightening because of what the stillness may bring to the surface.

If so, you may first need to create a safe place.

Begin to settle down, loosen, let go, forget, turn off the endless mental activity and emotional responses that keep you on the surface.

When you feel calmer, try to picture a place where you would like to be: a place where you feel welcome, accepted, and safe. This "safe place" could be by the ocean; it might be a room in your home, a friend's house, or a place you visited on vacation. Take some time to get grounded in that place. Notice what you see, hear, touch. Imagine Jesus coming to you in your safe place. Perhaps he takes you by the hand and leads you to a place where you can sit together. Perhaps he looks deeply into your eyes, and you into his.

As you relax, begin to say one of the following "breath prayers" with quiet intensity and relaxed concentration,

"Jesus, I worship you" (as you inhale), and "Touch my heart" (as you exhale).

"Jesus" (inhale), and "Come" (exhale).

"Heal me, Lord" (inhale), and "Hold me" (exhale).

This is a place to return to again and again. It is here, in time, that you may eventually be able to hand over the controls of your life to God, believing that he will indeed fulfill his promises to you.

Letting out the Pain

I stood at the door. It had been the longest two hours of my life. And the hardest. "Why hasn't God done something?" my friend asked, the tears washing her tired face. "I have tried so hard. I went to Chicago because of the pain center there. It was a joke. I tried the pain center in Boston. No one there could do anything. I have been prescribed all this pain medicine, which hasn't taken away the pain but made me feel numb. You saw me trying to get off all the morphine. It was awful.

"Now, after this last experience at the hospital, I can tell that the doctors there don't know what to do, either. They looked at my MRIs and suggested I try lifting weights to strengthen my muscles. Only Dr. Genson understood, but she's moving out of state. That was the last straw. It's like God is slapping me in the face every time I try to help myself. God doesn't care about me."

I wanted to tell my friend that God does care, that God can't do anything but love. But I knew she couldn't believe me. Twenty-five years of excruciating back pain—the result of a fall in her twenties—was compounded by her frustration, anger, and unfinished business from a tragic childhood.

She was speaking again. "Why did God put me in so many situations that ruined my life? Why didn't he protect me from my mom?"

"Not even your dad could do that, Jaciee."

"Then why did God do that to me?" she said, her tears a nonstop flood.

She had lost any hope of receiving a satisfactory answer. And, indeed, I had no answer to give. Instead, I felt anxious and restless. "I *should* have an answer," I heard an inner voice saying. "There is a doctor at the hospital I know. Maybe..."

Again my friend broke into my thoughts. "I feel like I'm clawing at the ground, trying to keep myself from sinking into an endless black whirlpool. I'm sorry I'm so out of control."

Something inside me cried out to her. "Jaciee, I know you don't want to hear this. But a little counseling could help."

No answer. She only cried harder. "I don't want to go through all my childhood issues again."

"I know," I gently responded.

After some time, Jaciee added quietly, "I don't want people to think this is all in my head. I'm afraid they won't believe me—that I really *am* in physical pain."

Again, I had no answer. She finally admitted, "I know I'm depressed. Chronic pain leads to depression. But I am afraid to open Pandora's box again. I'm sitting on the lid, because if I let it open up I know I won't be able to close it again. Ever."

"Jaciee, you won't be able to feel God's presence and love for you until you let the contents of that box out. I know it's scary. But you are putting up a wall between you and the deepest parts of yourself; then that wall goes up between you and your experience of God. But God is still there in your pain—even our walls can't keep him out. It's not that God's absent—you just can't sense him. You need to stop hiding."

"But if I let it out, it will just be another reminder of how bad I am." Jaciee's tears started again.

GOD DANCES FOR JOY at our birth, taking us in strong yet gentle arms as we enter into the world. As we encounter situations that are painful and deforming, God cries with us. He does not leave us alone in our pain, even when situations make us begin to close in on ourselves or induce us to hide from others, from ourselves, and from God. We are surrounded by the power and love of God, even in those moments when we feel God can't be trusted. We resist that love and set out on our own, fighting our way through life—or perhaps we feel that we're pitted against life, against ourselves, against God. Like Jaciee, we feel the need to take matters into our own hands.

Abraham, whose story is recounted within the first twenty-five chapters of Genesis, also felt he had to take matters into his own hands. The Lord promised him a glorious future: "I will make of you a great nation, and I will bless you, and make your name great, so that you will be a blessing" (Gen 12:2). So he and his beautiful wife pulled up their stakes, packed up their tents, and followed the Lord into a mysterious yet exciting future.

But as the years followed, even as the promise was reiterated and covenants with the Lord were sealed, no child appeared.

Though he was a man of faith, Abraham actually jeopardized the promise several times by manipulating circumstances so that the Lord's words might be fulfilled. Sarah said to her husband, "You see that the Lord has prevented me from bearing children; go in to my slave-girl; it may be that I shall obtain children by her" (Gen 16:3). Abraham tried to get a male descendant through Hagar—and, indeed, Hagar bore him a son whom he called Ishmael.

The Lord, however, kept on repeating the original promise, "You shall be the ancestor of a multitude of nations.... I will make you exceedingly fruitful; and I will make nations of you, and kings shall come from you" (Gen 17:4–5). And Abraham laughed. *How could this be?* he thought to himself. And yet, it *was* to be. Within a year Sarah bore him Isaac. She who was infertile bore a son to a man over a hundred years old. Isaac was the son of the promise, the boy through whom the blessings would be fulfilled.

Abraham's entire life was tied up with this child. On him rested every hope for the family's future. And, less than ten years later, it was *this* child that God asked Abraham to sacrifice on the mountain in the land of Moriah.[1]

"So Abraham rose early in the morning, saddled his donkey, and took two of his young men with him, and his son Isaac...and set out and went to the place in the distance that God had shown him" (Gen 22:3). It seems incredible. How could Abraham, who for years had been manipulating events to protect the promise the Lord had made to him, now, without a word, simply get up at the Lord's voice and go?

Unbeknownst to him, the Lord was not asking Abraham for his son's life. It was *Abraham's* life that the Lord still wanted, Abraham's trust that he still had not received. *Abraham,* the Lord was asking, *can you let me take your life into my hands? Will you entrust your entire life and future unconditionally to me, now when it seems everything has ended?* "I will indeed bless you, and I will make your offspring as numerous as the stars of heaven and as the sand that is on the seashore" (Gen 22:17). *Abraham, are you able to trust me yet?*

And Abraham rose early in the morning and set out.... Abraham finally handed everything over to God. Even at the painful prospect of losing this son, who meant more than everything to him, Abraham was ready now to believe. He had finally learned to give up control over his own life. Abraham had finally learned that life is authentic only when it is received as a gift, as grace.

When we hand our lives over to the Lord, we come out of hiding—hiding behind *our* ideas of how things should be, hiding behind who *we* think we are, hiding behind *our* dreams for our future. As God showed himself faithful when Abraham stepped out in faith with Isaac at his side, God showed himself faithful to Jaicee, and will manifest his fidelity to anyone who takes a trusting step into the unknown.

Be Still

⮑ *Wisdom to guide you:* "But I foresee your question: If this or that other thing happens, what will become of me? Let this be your attitude: ...to live in absolute dependence upon God, to live day by day, from hour to hour, from moment to moment without concerning myself with either tomorrow or future generally. Tomorrow will take care of itself.... Let us rely solely upon his Fatherly care; let us surrender ourselves to it utterly for all our temporal and spiritual and even our eternal welfare."

Jean-Pierre de Caussade[2]

～ *Scripture to hold you:* When the cares of my heart are many, your consolations, Lord, lift my heart (cf. Ps 94:19).

～ *Thought to sustain you:* God and I commit ourselves to be faithful to each other.

STEP THREE

Risking Trust

EVEN BEFORE MAKING PEACE with ourselves, most of us probably would like to "see" God, to have proof that he is really there, *really there* for us. We aren't so ready to give God the benefit of the doubt. It's too risky—we know very well how much blind trust can cost. No, we want to *see* God's radiant face shining on us. If God shows up and proves true to who he says he is, *then* we will surely believe in him.

Close your eyes. Take a quick scan of your body, starting with the crown of your head all the way down to your feet. Tell each part of your body to relax.

With each breath drawn in, say: *peace*. With each breath let out, say: *light*.

Let go of everything: memories, ideas, dreams, worries, plans. Let go of noises, voices, people. Let there only be *now*. Come into the present moment.

In your imagination, go to your safe place. Spend some time there, deepening your sense of peace.

Begin to pray very softly, leaving periods of silence between the phrases:

There is nothing I am waiting for, Lord. There is nothing I expect.

You see I am here in this place of warmth and safety.

I am alone.

I am told you are here, too. I cannot feel you. I cannot see you.

I can't even be sure if you are listening to me.

But I bow down, nevertheless, and I adore you.

You are my God.

You are forever.

You are all.

You are darkness and light.

You are nearby and far away.

You are present in the stars and you are in every cell of my body.

You are the beginning and the end.

You are invisible. You are safe.

You are strength.

You are patience.

You are beauty.

You are gentleness.

You are the fury of truth that will not back down.

You are the tenderness of love that will never end.

I cannot see you. I cannot feel you. I don't know what you look like or what you think of me. That doesn't really matter. What is important to me right now is that I adore you because you are God. You are my Creator. You keep me in existence. Yours are the first eyes I will see when I awake after death. It is important to me to adore you, even if today I may not be able to love you.

Remain in silence. Accept whatever you are feeling: peace, anger, resistance, bitterness, joy, hope, or excitement. Let the feelings rise and fall until there is silence.

Then pray: *One day, show me your glory, Lord. Amen.*

The Experience of the Inexpressible

I met him on retreat. I was a member of the retreat team, he a retreatant with all the enthusiasm and glow of someone who had just found the fountain of eternity. Antonio, an Italian man in his fifties, gave the appearance that he would be more at home in his brother's corner café in a village of Tuscany than in a retreat house in the United States. He had a lot to say—too much, some thought. Indeed, a silent retreat probably taxed Antonio to the limit. As I set the table for the final celebratory meal that ended the retreat, Antonio shared with me not only his story, but also the nuggets of wisdom he had gleaned from his years of searching for peace.

"One day, just as I came home from confession, my son did something that irritated me, and I got upset." Antonio covered his head with his hands. *"I can't believe it,* I said to myself. *I just went to confession and I've already screwed up again."* Thinking his problem was not having made a really complete confession, Antonio enlisted the prayers of some nuns and then made another appointment for the sacrament of Reconciliation. He wanted this liturgical moment to be *the* confession that would mark the end of one life and the beginning of another.

"Afterward, however, I still didn't feel any different," Antonio continued. "In fact, I was as impatient and irritated with my children as before. *What is wrong with me?* I asked myself. One Sunday after Mass, I stopped to speak with the priest. I explained to him the situation and he asked me one question, 'But did you repent?' A light went on. That's it! I had gone to confession, but I hadn't repented! I wasn't willing to take the concrete steps needed to change my life. I wasn't willing to undergo a 100 percent conversion. And, Sister," he said solemnly, "when you ask God for the 100 percent, you'd better be careful, because God answers your prayer—he brings you the whole way.

"It's like this. You start to pray, you get going in the spiritual life, you become better, and you reach a plateau around 30 percent. Then you say, 'Hey, I've worked hard. This is pretty good. I feel better. I feel close to God. I'm going to stay right here.' And what happens is you just level off, you never go for the 100 percent. There is something about the plateau we like; we'd rather keep up part of our unrepentant lifestyle. We don't really want to let God ask for total surrender, a complete and continuous change of heart. But if we tell God we want to go the whole way, then...." Again his words were replaced by a radiant smile that expressed his experience of the inexpressible.

Antonio was unable to find the words, but I knew what he meant. When you tell God, "I give you everything," God takes it all. And in doing so, God frees you from yourself. Even when you feel grief or pain over what you have relinquished, you will find you have gained so much more than what you lost.

As the time for a final group sharing arrived, I learned more about Antonio's wisdom as we concluded our conversation.

"When we first take our Christian discipleship seriously and commit ourselves to accountability with other Christians who are doing the same, we find out that we have a lot of rough edges. Our personality is harsh, or we're sharp in the way we relate to others, or we're a bit out of shape in our prayer. But it is the process of following Christ that helps us to go deeper and deeper into ourselves so that we empty ourselves: prayer, the sacraments, commitment to a group, or spiritual direction. We empty ourselves completely so that Jesus can take up residence more fully within us. Jesus changes our sharp edges and makes us gentle. It's a practical thing. It's working with God in a real way. It requires sincerity, and once we love the truth above everything, God sets us free. That's communion."

~

ANOTHER MAN'S FACE had worn the radiance of the inexpressible One. His name was Moses. Moses had the often-thankless job of leading the Israelites out of slavery in Egypt, back to the land God had given Abraham and his descendants over four hundred years earlier. This land was to have been their perpetual possession, yet when famine later struck the world, Jacob (Abraham's grandson, renamed Israel) and his entire family fled their homeland to Egypt. There Joseph, Jacob's son with the big dreams and multicolored coat, had ended up after his brothers had sold him into slavery. The young man had climbed the ranks of power quickly after correctly interpreting Pharaoh's unsettling dreams foreshadowing a worldwide famine. Through Joseph's preparation, the people survived. Jacob and his family were given refuge, later settling in Egypt. As generations passed and the Israelites increased, however, they became enslaved by the Egyptians; their manual work supplied the manpower for Egypt's immense architectural projects.

God had other plans for his people. Moses was to obtain their release from Egypt and lead them back to their own land. But the Hebrews were a "stiff-necked people," fickle in their love for and loyalty to the God who had rescued them from bondage. Over and over again Moses interceded for the people before Yahweh, and in the rough-and-tumble of

his own relationship with the Lord, the two became the closest of friends. When Moses came down from the mountain
after speaking with Yahweh or left the tent of meeting, his
face shone with a radiance no one else could bear to look
upon. The glory of his countenance expressed his privileged
place as a servant close to Yahweh.

> One day, Moses took the risk of asking the LORD for a
> vision of his glory.
>   Moses said, "Show me your glory, I pray." ...And the
> LORD continued, "See, there is a place by me where you
> shall stand on the rock; and while my glory passes by I will
> put you in a cleft of the rock, and I will cover you with my
> hand until I have passed by; then I will take away my hand,
> and you shall see my back; but my face shall not be seen."
> The LORD descended in the cloud and stood with him
> there, and proclaimed the name, "The LORD." The LORD
> passed before him, and proclaimed, "The LORD, the LORD,
> a God merciful and gracious, slow to anger, and abounding
> in steadfast love and faithfulness." (Ex 33:18–23; 34:5–6)

Although he had continual experiences of intimacy with
the Lord, Moses always remained unsatisfied. He even
asked the Lord for his friendship, as if he hadn't received
any sign of the Lord's love before. Gregory of Nyssa, in his
Life of Moses, defines the vision of God as "never to be
satisfied in the desire to see him."[1]

Gregory wrote of Moses' request to see God's glory,
"Indeed he [God] would not have shown himself to his
servant if the vision would have been such as to terminate
Moses's desire; for the true vision of God consists rather in
this, that the soul that looks up to God never ceases to desire
him...."[2]

Spirituality, both for Antonio and Gregory of Nyssa, is
growth. Antonio affirms, "Conversion isn't a one-time thing.
It happens over and over again. It takes a commitment–then

you know healing of the heart and grace lift us up." It is going from step to step, from glory to glory, in a continuous movement toward greater faith, hope, and love. Sin can be defined as a refusal to grow. God, on the other hand, is an infinite horizon always beckoning us further into the Divine Majesty. Communion with God is a constant ascent from "glory to glory." With each step, we joyously expect something more. Perfection is lived, therefore, when the only thing worthy of honor and desire is for us to become God's friends, and when falling from God's friendship is the worst thing that could befall us.

Be Still

〜 *Wisdom to guide you:* "I am not always faithful, but I am never discouraged; I leave myself wholly in the arms of our Divine Lord; he teaches me to draw from all–both good and ill that he finds in me. He teaches me to speculate in the Bank of Love, or rather it is he who acts for me without telling me how he goes to work; that is his affair and not mine; my part is complete surrender, reserving nothing to myself, not even the gratification of knowing how my credit stands with the Bank."

St. Thérèse of Lisieux[3]

〜 *Scripture to hold you:* "Those who love me will keep my word, and my Father will love them, and we will come to them and make our home with them" (Jn 14:23).

〜 *Thought to sustain you:* Show me your glory, Lord, I pray.

Exploring Inner Prisons

IN PRAYER WE DESIRE to be progressively transformed into who we really are before the face of God who truly *is*. This may or may not change our outer situation, but as we remain in God's presence, our inner being shines with that radiance. And through varying circumstances, everyone (including ourselves) can see God loving into existence our most authentic self, the person he created us to be.

Spend some time in silent prayer and personal discovery. Begin by quieting your heart and soul in God's presence, reaffirming, "Say to the fearful, 'Be strong, do not fear!'" (cf. Isa 35:4). Repeat this verse of Scripture softly several times, allowing it to settle deep into your heart. Then continue.

Using the image of a prison, explore imprisoning situations you have lived through or are currently living in. These situations could have been created by someone's attitudes toward you; a situation of injustice or abuse; events in your childhood; your own fears or shyness; a financial or physical tragedy; a betrayal, etc. What have been your imprisoning situations?

Taking each situation in turn, write about your prison and how it feels to be in it. What does it look like? Who else is there? How does it affect your life? Who else is affected? Is God with you in that prison at all, or do you feel all alone?

Reflecting on these imprisoning situations, you may become aware of certain "life lessons" that were impressed upon you over the years. These "life lessons" may have seemed helpful for a time, but may be obstacles to growth and maturity at this point in your life. Write these down as well. For example, perhaps your "prison experience" led you to conclude that:

- you should not exist;
- if you don't conform you are bad;
- you are worthless;
- you should not grow up or be successful;
- intimacy is not safe;
- you must not dream.

These injunctions became signposts to survival. We came to believe that, in order to be accepted or loved, we needed to:

- disappear,
- not think,
- conform,
- remain a child, or
- protect ourselves from love.

Thus, we began to shut off the truest part of who we are. Unconsciously, we began to make decisions that would ensure survival:

Since I am not acceptable as I am, I must not think for myself or disagree. I must always do what the other person wants.

Since my parents loved me only as long as I remained a child, I choose to remain a child and not grow up.

Since it is "bad" to be happy and spontaneous, I have decided to be sad. Only then will I be (in a twisted way) "good."

What are the injunctions you learned? List them.

What situations or behaviors in your present life are being affected by these injunctions?

Take a few moments to thank God for your life and for the ways God has been there, seeing you through each year, each event, each relationship. You may wish to share this experience with a friend or trusted guide.

I Await Love

We met in prison. In the twenty minutes we were allowed together, Mena's story unfolded. Mena, the young mother of four children, had been hanging out with a group of young adults, not fully realizing that they were hoping to make a little extra money off a "harmless" sale of drugs. But the situation turned out to be anything but harmless. People were hurt, and Mena was arrested with the group.

Tears flowed freely as she told of her humiliation, of the pain only a mother could know. In the two years she had been incarcerated, Mena's four children had drifted away from her. At first she had wanted her children to visit her in prison. She desperately wanted to see them. She invited them. She encouraged them to come. She so wanted to make up to them all they were missing because of her absence as she waited for her case to go to court. Her oldest daughter came at first, but after a while, the frequency of her visits fell off. But the youngest, only seven years old, never came.

Mena said, "I had to realize they have lives of their own, lives they need to live right now. I can't be with them during these years. And it is so hard. But I also have to think of what *they* need." It was clear that these were hard words to say and even harder to accept.

Those first months in prison were angry, desperate months for Mena. She wanted out. She was angry at herself for being so naïve, for getting involved in something so stupid. "But if I had known what I have learned here before I discovered drugs, I wouldn't be behind bars. After the chaplain recommended a neurological workup, I started taking medication that has left me feeling so stable and able to think through situations. Now my goals in life have changed," she said. "I have been here longer than all the other women in this section of prison. My case hasn't even gone to court, and I'm still here. Since I'm the oldest one, I take the new ones under my wing and try to help them out. You know why? One day I realized that if I can't love the people I'm with right now, every day—if I can't be Jesus for them—then I won't be able to love, really love my family when I am released. So that's how I'm spending my life now."

Instinctively I knew that Mena was sharing with me the deepest truth of who she was becoming. "I was wrong. Even if it wasn't entirely planned, I should have known better. I was wrong to be with that group. I am not trying to escape responsibility." Her tears were not of anger or of discouragement. They were the honest tears of one who has touched the core of her being and become truly alive. "I believe that Jesus is giving me this time; it's time to grow into a better person. Every day now I pray and I try to help others. I want to serve them and show them that they are lovable, too."

Mena reminded me of another young adult, also a parent, who lived in Paris, France. On February 25, 1954, in the Rue Vivienne in Paris, Jacques Fesch assaulted and robbed a moneychanger of the money he needed to escape a personally intolerable situation. As he fled the attempted robbery, he was stopped by the police and, in the altercation, Fesch killed an officer. At his trial, he was condemned to death by guillotine.

At first he refused to see a chaplain. But at the end of his first year in prison, Fesch wrote, "A powerful wave of emotion swept over me, causing deep and brutal suffering. Within the space of a few hours, I came into possession of faith, with absolute certainty. I believed, and could no longer understand how I had ever not believed. Grace had come to me. A great joy flooded my soul, and above all a deep peace. In a few instants everything had become clear. It was a very strong, sensible joy that I felt."[1]

On the night of his conversion, Jacques Fesch heard an interior voice urging him to convert. He listened to that voice, which led him over the next three years to ever greater joy, for he would never cease to listen to it. Less than a month before his execution, he wrote, "I am living through marvelous hours, and I feel as if I had never lived any other life than the one I've been experiencing for a month now. Jesus draws me to Himself, and knowing the weakness of my soul He gives me much, while asking for so little. For each small effort that I make I receive another grace, and, in view of the shortness of the time, this ascent toward God is being achieved far more quickly than it would be for someone who still had years ahead of him."[2]

The last sentence in Jacques' journal is: "I wait in the dark, and in peace.... I await Love!"[3] On October 1, 1957, after he and his lawyer received Communion, Jacques was executed.

~

MENA AND JACQUES can stand as icons of life—life with its complex twists and turns, the blows it deals us, the mistakes we can't erase, and yet, with its ultimate reliability. No biblical character emerges as such an icon more than David.

David was anointed heir to the throne by the prophet Samuel and grew up in the court of Saul, later becoming a military and political genius. Out of jealousy, King Saul attempted to kill David, so David and his men took refuge in a cave. When King Saul set up camp in the same cave, David refused to seize the opportunity to kill the king. "The Lord forbid that I should do this thing to my lord, the Lord's anointed, to raise my hand against him" (1 Sam 24:6). The sincerity and magnanimity of David's act is only one of many examples that establish David's honor as the ideal of fidelity to the Lord. Yet, David also had a darker side. When the sheepherder Nabal refused to give David and his men food after they had protected his herds, it was only Nabal's wife, Abigail, who saved the surly Nabal and his entire household from destruction at the hands of David the warlord. The beautiful and clever Abigail pacified David, prostrating herself on the ground before him and giving his men the food they needed. After Nabal's death just a few days later, David married Abigail, now a wealthy landowner, and consolidated his power. And, of course, David's bloodthirsty ambition is revealed further in the famous incident of the murder of Uriah so that he could marry Uriah's beautiful wife, Bathsheba (cf. 2 Sam 11–12).

So why did God love David so much? Despite David's flaws and weaknesses, the Bible clearly shows that God constantly protected him and the dynasty that he founded. David was not perfect, but God's fidelity and promise never wavered. David sinned, often seriously, but he never forsook his primary loyalty to the Lord. The Scriptures remind us that the meaning of both his successes and failures was not that David deserved the praise, but that God had chosen to use the weak king to accomplish his divine purpose. The Bible sees David through God's eyes.

Both Mena and Jacques also discovered those eyes. They stopped fighting the consequences of their actions, slowed down, and experienced in a powerful way what few of us really know: the compassion of God.

God makes himself vulnerable in loving us, drawing close enough to us that we can see ourselves in *God's* eyes. We so easily turn away from God's gaze through guilt, through anger, through egoism. Perhaps we don't want God to look at us because we think we are ugly, we are failures, we are sinners. But if we allow God's gaze to arrest our own through grace, we just might be able to admit what we have done, to be forgiven, and forgive ourselves, accept the consequences, and surrender to what God desires to accomplish in our lives.

Gods' will always lays itself open to the mistakes, the waywardness, the rebelliousness of humanity, that God may lead humanity to free consent. In this way, God teaches us, mentors us, trains us. God waits at our side as a beggar of love, never forcing our response, but he is always there, always waiting, always loving.

Be Still

〰 *Wisdom to guide you:* "As for me, I glorify you in making known how good you are to sinners, and that your mercy prevails over all malice, that nothing can destroy it, that no matter how many times, or how shamefully we fall, or how criminally, a sinner need not be driven to despair of your pardon.... It is in vain that your enemy and mine sets new traps for me every day. He will make me lose everything else before the hope that I have in your mercy."

St. Claude de la Colombiere[4]

〰 *Scripture to hold you:* "I received mercy because I had acted ignorantly in unbelief, and the grace of our Lord overflowed for me with the faith and love that are in Christ Jesus" (1 Tim 1:13–16).

〰 *Thought to sustain you:* You, O God, are always by my side, always waiting, always loving.

Discovering Compassion

YOUR HEART CALLS out for healing. The illusions, fright-ened agendas, and compensations that have kept you in prison until now have been exposed; they no longer have power over you. Another way is possible to you now: to live from the deepest part of yourself, where you truly are God's dream. You are far more than the survival tactics, masks, and defenses you have unconsciously developed to protect yourself. Until now, it may have been the only way you could survive. This isn't true anymore.

In a place of prayer, or with a friend or spiritual guide, read over the imprisoning situations you wrote about in the last exercise. Think or speak about the times or situations in your present life that have been influenced by the survival tactics you pinpointed in that exercise. With great gentleness, accept what you are feeling. The dissatisfaction, fear, sense of isolation, lack of authenticity, or the presence of guilt.

It is time to purify these survival mechanisms and to progressively free yourself from their control.

Very quietly, begin to center yourself with your breathing. You may use a word to focus your attention: "peace,"
"let it be," "yes."

If you wish, picture yourself in a situation that is causing
you distress. Jesus comes to stand by your side. He takes
your hand or puts his arm around you. You are not alone
anymore. Then read these thoughts slowly, taking time to
let them penetrate your heart:

*I have suffered enough doing what others want in order to buy their
love or acceptance. I have suffered enough for not being myself.*

My love, my life, my dreams have been distorted and falsified.

*Now I can begin again, from this point. I have brought everything
to the light, put everything on the table. I can leave behind every ideal-
ized image of myself. I can live now from the depths of my being,
because only in this way can I give and receive true love.*

Turn toward Jesus and away from persons or events that
have caused you pain. Look into Jesus' face and see the
compassion and strength in his eyes. Jesus has always
known your heart's goodness. In his eyes you were always
worth loving, always beautiful—that fact has never changed.

The suffering in your life can yield great treasures. It is
possible to find gifts in the ashes, treasures in the flames. But
don't worry about that now. Jesus himself will show you
where the gold lies. You only need to hold on to him, to lean
in your weakness on his power, to trust in your poverty on
his bountiful love. Lay your head down on his heart and rest
as a little child sleeps in his or her parent's arms.

When you are ready, gently return to the room in which
you are praying. If you are sharing this exercise with a friend
or guide, you may wish to go over what happened between
Jesus and yourself, speaking about any feelings or words or
impressions that may have come to you.

Lost in the Shuffle

The other day Laura shared with me her memories of her mother. Laura was one of five children; her mother was a well-respected employee in a government office in their hometown. Laura remembered how happy her mother was with her working environment. A personnel management specialist, she had received training in mine engineering.

She noticed that the engineers often lost a lot of time searching through volumes of regulations and laws regarding mining projects. So she studied the books herself, and very soon individuals both in and outside her department were tapping into her expertise. Recognizing her capabilities, her boss soon began to ask her to travel to meetings in other locations. She also received many awards for initiating new ideas that benefited everyone in the department. Those were fulfilling and happy years for her.

However, five years before her retirement, her boss told her he was being transferred to another state and wanted her to ask for a transfer also, which would mean moving her entire family. It was impossible. Instead, she remained behind and trained the new boss.

The arrival of this new boss brought a new chapter in her life. Though she put at his disposal all the knowledge she had gained, he repaid her generosity by using her to get himself ahead. Gradually he began to take work away from her and assign the tasks to other employees. He criticized the work she did until she was trusted only with simple secretarial tasks. Laura's mother never understood why her new boss was so unhappy with her, and during the months in which she tried to work with him, the department became more and more unbearable for her and her co-workers. At home she expressed her frustration in tears.

Encouraged by friends and family who believed in her gifts, Laura's mom saw these voices as lights in the darkness, given to her from an all-seeing and loving God. Strengthened by prayer and an openness to combat negative influences with positive actions, Laura's mom began to take pleasure in doing even the little things she was still permitted to do. She created for herself new outlets that to others might have seemed insignificant: arriving early in order to make coffee for her fellow workers, dividing mail and getting it ready for pickup. She still fulfilled her regular secretarial work, but now with a new purpose—love.

ANOTHER WOMAN—I'll call her Joann—has also inspired me with her strength and courage in facing situations of injustice. Before I met her, Joann was married, had three wonderful girls, and enjoyed the good things in life. Then the domestic abuse began. Over the years, as her husband's violence against her escalated, she was caught in the typical cycle of abuse. When she finally fled with her three children, they escaped with only the clothes they had on.

For three months Joann lived with her girls in a shelter. She had to find a job, a home, a new school for her girls.... All the while she was scared and exhausted. The legal part of the divorce was ugly and corrupt, stripping her of hundreds of thousands of dollars that should legally have been hers. During one of our chats, Joann used an image that has stuck with me: "It is like I'm trying to play the game Candyland by Monopoly's rules. It just doesn't work."

"That's such a marvelous image, Joann," I replied. "The choices you have made for your daughters' lives and safety, the way Jesus has been for you the only source of solace and strength in these years, are an image of the Kingdom of God—a Candyland image of sweets and gifts and joy. They may not mean a whole lot in a competitive 'Monopoly' world, but the Kingdom of God that is coming about also through your choices is much more important than Monopoly. It will last forever. In the end, it is the poor who have been ripped off in this world who will be first, and those who are first now will be last."

JUDITH IS A WOMAN often lost in the shuffle of the pages of Scripture. A quiet widow devoted to prayer and an upright life, she possessed tremendous strength. To that strength she united the "littleness" of one who lives in adoration of God. The Book of Judith tells of her courage and trust in God when her hometown was under siege.

The general Holofernes and his army had besieged the Israelite city of Bethulia. There was no escape for the Israelites. As their families began to starve inside the city walls, they cried out to the Lord their God and demanded that their leaders surrender to Holofernes.

The leaders answered the people, "Courage. Let us hold out for five more days, for God will have mercy on us. But *if he doesn't come to help us,* we shall surrender as you say."

Judith, a respected and pious widow, heard about what the leaders had said. She summoned them to her and told them that their plan was not right. "Who are you to put God to the test today, and to set yourselves up in the place of God in human affairs? You are putting the Lord Almighty to the test" (Jdt 8:12ff.).

With courage she continued, "For if he does not choose to help us within these five days, he has power to protect us within any time he pleases, or even to destroy us in the presence of our enemies.... In spite of everything let us give thanks to the Lord our God, who is putting us to the test as he did our ancestors" (Jdt 8:15, 25).

When the officials of Bethulia left her, Judith prostrated herself in prayer, then dressed herself in festive attire and anointed herself with perfume. She was very beautiful, and the rulers of the town were astounded. "Open the gates!" Judith requested, and she slipped out with her maid, walking firmly into enemy territory, though she knew not exactly what the Lord was going to accomplish through her.

Taken into custody by the Assyrian patrol, Judith told them that she was fleeing the Hebrews and on her way to see Holofernes. She was immediately taken to the general's tent and remained there for three days. Each evening she went out to pray, and she ate only of the provisions she had brought with her. On the fourth day, Holofernes held a banquet for his attendants and called Judith to be a part of the festivities. During the meal he was entranced by Judith's beauty. He also drank a large amount of wine.

When evening came, Holofernes's attendants withdrew, leaving Judith alone in his tent. The commander was stretched out on his bed, dead drunk. Standing beside his bed, Judith prayed to the Lord for help. Then she took down the sword that hung on Holofernes's bedpost and struck him twice, cutting off his head. Quickly she put his head in a bag and went out as usual to pray. She and her maid passed through the camp and returned to Bethulia.

"Open," she called out. "Open the gate! God is with us!" All the people were astonished. They bowed down and worshiped God. The shout that came from the Israelites' town was so great that all the soldiers in the enemy encampments jumped to attention. When they went to call their commander, they discovered Holofernes' death. Overcome with fear, they did not wait for one another but fled across the plain and through the hill country.

While the rulers of Bethulia had seen death around them, Judith had told them that they needed to believe that God sought only to give them life.

I can't count the number of times I have heard, "God didn't do what I asked when I needed him most. I gave God enough chances. How can I trust him anymore?" To make peace with ourselves, sometimes we need to make peace with God, reconciling ourselves to the fact that no matter what we see around us, God wants life for us and God *is* accomplishing our good.

The difference between Judith and the leaders of Bethulia is important. Bethulia's leaders and people were looking out for themselves. Judith, however, was looking at God; she understood that, ultimately, the victory and glory belong to God alone. And so she—like Laura's mother and like Joann—sought to glorify God at every moment, from within every situation in which she found herself.

Although Judith prayed and stated her dependence on God, she didn't sit around helplessly awaiting the inevitable. She made herself an instrument in God's hands for the salvation of his people, setting out from Bethulia, across the valley, and into Holofernes' camp without a detailed plan of action. In so doing, she made herself even more vulnerable than the rest of her people. She left the safety of the city walls and went alone, accompanied only by her maid—hardly a means of defense.

She was a woman entering a man's world, without protection, with only a prayer. A civilian among soldiers.

The human tendency would be to provide for protection and backup, just in case. Judith, however, gave up whatever protection she had and walked into the hands of the Lord. Laura's mother and Joann, in examples much closer to our own experience, did the same. They *acted* on the belief that God was bringing about life in their situations, no matter how dark they seemed. These women took risks not on human but on divine possibilities.

Be Still

〜 *Wisdom to guide you:* "I thank my Jesus for making me walk in darkness; in it I am wrapped in profound peace. Willingly I consent to stay, during my...life, in this somber tunnel into which he has made me enter. I desire only that my darkness may win light for sinners."

St. Thérèse of Lisieux[1]

〜 *Scripture to hold you:* "Call on me in the day of trouble; I will deliver you and you shall glorify me" (Ps 50:15).

〜 *Thought to sustain you:* I walk into your hands, O Lord.

PART TWO

Healing

Tell Me

Tell me all your troubles, tell me all your fears.
Tell me now what makes you sad, and I'll wipe dry
    your tears.
For once I too felt this same pain
in a garden, by a friend I too was betrayed.
Has your love been slighted? Has it been abused?
Have you ever felt that your friendship was used?
And yes, I too had such a friend.
When he kissed me, I was seized and led to my death.
Are you feeling lonely, are you feeling down?
Do you feel that true friends are nowhere to be found?
Yes, once I too felt lonely.
In a courtroom, those I loved turned their backs on me.
Does your heart feel heavy under the burden
of your worries, cares, and needs, past enduring?
Yes, once I too was under the weight
of a cross upon my back—the pain was so great.
Are you feeling guilty? Have you done wrong?
Let me take you in my arms, for my love is strong.
Yes, on the cross I died for you.
Now I'll help you rise and walk—your life is renewed.

Choosing Directions

SETTLE INTO A PLACE of prayer, either alone or with a trust-ed companion. Take a moment to notice the characteristics of the space. Are you inside or outside? What are the sounds around you? Why did you choose this place? Are there objects or pictures that make it particularly meaning-ful? Or is it a bare place, like a desert, which in its simplici-ty receives you as you are?

Next scan your interior space. How are you feeling? What are your expectations? Do you have any anxiety about this time of prayer and interior liberation? Scan your body, from your feet to your head, and tell yourself to relax. Allow the silence to wash over you, wrapping itself around you with its comforting arms. Repeat quietly and reverently the phrase: "Be still now. God is here."

Let yourself slip deeper and deeper. Picture that place within yourself where God calls you by name. It may be a lush green field full of wildflowers, or a sanctuary that breathes divine presence.

In this place you can let go of all your masks and defen-ses. Here you are completely loved. Here, where God pronounces your name, you can be truly happy. You no longer need to "buy" happiness and acceptance.

Here, in this place, love expands more and more, taking over your thoughts and fears, replacing your attitudes and words and perceptions. Here you are peace. You are filled with light that comes from God, who is Love and Goodness itself. It is certain and true: You are the outpouring of God's immensely tender love, which is always just beginning, always expanding and opening itself, always spreading light, always bestowing life.

Take a few moments to breathe in this light. Breathe in light and breathe out any darkness you may feel. Breathe in light and breathe out attitudes that mar the perfection of that crystalline brightness. Breathe in light, which permeates every cell of your body, and breathe out feelings that are obstacles to that light.

You are also a gift for others. Through you as through a channel, God wishes to give gifts to others. Only in this way, in giving love away, you are truly and most deeply yourself.

This way represents a new decision, a new place, a new direction in life, a new beginning. By choosing to live contrary to your survival strategies, you give authentic life and love to others. By choosing laughter and joy, you say no to the lies that blocked your life. In loving, you will come to know yourself deeply.

Remain a while in the joy of finally being able to be who you are. Soak in the possibilities of new beginnings and new directions.[1]

I Have Offered You Freedom

One day I received a letter from a gentleman in Illinois. "I thought that someone might be able to use this story," he wrote, "and so I sent it to you." Thus began one of those connections God establishes to multiply his grace and mercy.

In his letter, Patrick described a difficult time in his life. "Jesus, I love you. Jesus, I love you." It was the only prayer Patrick could say. He had forgotten all the other prayers he had learned as a boy. This one short plea to God, however, had become his lifeboat in a sea of disappointments and misery. It was a simple prayer, simple and desperate.

The seven months in which Patrick uttered this prayer almost with every breath were not easy ones. They were marked by divorce, loss of a beautiful home, business failure, and loneliness. Patrick couldn't understand why his life had turned so sour. He continued to say, "Jesus, I love you. Jesus, I love you," though it seemed such a contradiction. Where was this God who could change things? Why hadn't God intervened? Was Patrick being punished—and, if so, what terrible thing had he done to deserve all this? The questions kept coming as fast as Patrick could say his prayer. They were not questions of anger; they were questions of wanting to understand, wanting to communicate with the only One who could help him.

By this time, Patrick was living in his van. Periodically, members of the parish would take him in for a night or two and give him a hot meal. Such nights were a respite in his otherwise complete isolation. As the weeks wore on, Patrick began to notice something. Even though he had lost just about everything he loved and possessed, he now had something new: peace and contentment. It was an odd feeling to be so broken and yet so much at peace. It made no sense. He worried about where his life would go next, what life "beyond the van" would be like. And yet, Patrick also seemed to be held up by invisible supports.

One night, Patrick felt a pain in his chest so severe he thought he was having a heart attack. He managed to drive himself to the hospital. The doctor who examined him told him he was in perfect health.

"Then what is this pain I feel?" he asked the doctor.

"Probably the stress of your situation," the doctor replied.

Two days later Patrick was in a parishioner's home, watching TV with the family after supper. Again he felt the pain in his chest. A tingling feeling, warm and deep, seemed to wrap itself around his heart. It lasted only a few seconds. When the tingling left him, the pain was gone.

The next day a man from the parish prayer group came up to Patrick—he had to deliver a message from Jesus. Patrick wasn't into receiving messages from Jesus through other people, but the man got his attention when Patrick realized he had received the message at the same time he had felt the tingling in his chest.

These were the words that Jesus had wanted delivered to Patrick: "My child, you seek a quick answer to a longstanding problem. You seek the glory of the Risen Christ without taking up your cross. My child, you walk still attached to this world, even though I have offered you freedom from all its fetters.

"My child, you expect all without any concerted effort on your part. This will not be the case, my son. You will have to come to me by way of the cross.

"Accept the cross with a joyful heart, accept the cross with praise on your lips. Walk in complete trust in me. Despise your life in this world, and all that it offers.

"Give me complete control of every aspect of your life, even your very breath and heartbeat. I seek this freedom from you, this surrender by you.

"This will be the starting place to new freedom and healing for you. This will give me the freedom to heal the unforgiveness that is still pent up in you.

"My son, do you not feel the unforgiveness festering in you? Let it go with all your heart. Learn to trust completely in me. If I should subject you to death, then accept it with a joyful heart because you have given me your all, and this is what I ask. There should be nothing in this world that should bring you unrest. I am in total control.

"My child, why do you value this world so much? What has it given you, that you hold it so dear to your heart? Let it go and seek only oneness with me. Walk not in fear but in peace and joy with me. I offer myself to you for strength and insight and healing. It is a gift found in the cross. Walk totally with me, my son, not by the words from your lips but by the witness of your cross."

SOMETIMES WE BARGAIN with God, seeking to buy security with our prayers, our religious activities, or our righteous behavior.

"I give to the missions, why should this happen to me?"

"What have I done to deserve this? I go to church every Sunday."

"Why is it that people get away with murder, and this happens to *me*?"

"This isn't fair!"

We discover in time, however, that God cannot be bought—he loves us too much to be caught up in our anxious games. We have a tendency to seek the good things of life and to blame God for anything bad that happens to ourselves or our loved ones. Once we have pulled things together—house, family, career, financial security—anything that upsets the balance must be remedied as quickly as possible. Things need to return to the way they *were*.

We are afraid of change. But our God is a God of the future, a God walking always into the unknown *with us*.

The Book of Isaiah has a long and complex history—four hundred years, extending from the eighth to the fifth centuries before the birth of Christ. The prophet Isaiah is associated with the first thirty-nine oracles of the book, and his disciples and anonymous prophets account for the oracles in the rest of the book.

The prophecies of the Book of Isaiah paint the catastrophic history of Israel in broad strokes. The prophecies juxtapose condemnation and salvation, distress and restoration, waywardness and fidelity, upheaval and peace. They seem to be random prophetic fragments, but on closer reading this chaotic collection reflects the events of history and even the events of our own life. The prophet deals with the bewildering mystery of the rise and fall of events that are an enigma to us. He asks and answers questions we all ask:

Why is it that the unjust person flourishes?

Why do good people suffer?

Where is God when tragedy strikes?

How could God let that tsunami kill so many people?

How can one man get away with creating so much destruction for the people in his country?

Why did God answer my prayer for a new house, only to let me lose my job a year later?

The confusing sequence of life's events is a bewildering mystery.

Isaiah helps us "see" and "hear" the supreme drama of history and life on a deeper level. He shares the same questions we have. He, too, wonders at the purposes of God. But fundamentally, Isaiah believes that there is more to history than historians describe, more to our lives than what we perceive. History is more than the collective decisions of presidents and activity of soldiers; it is more than the fluctuations of the dollar and the suffering of people. Our lives are more than the jobs we have or lose, the money we save, the tragedies we survive. At its deepest level, history—whether that of a nation or that of a person—is about the relationship between God and us.

The supreme drama is therefore that God's word meets with our refusal. We forget all that God did for our ancestors—our biblical mothers and fathers, the saints, and those who have witnessed to us God's power and fidelity. Because we have forgotten God's covenant with us, we are unable to decipher the code of history: We have eyes, but do not see, ears, but do not hear.

According to Isaiah, *forgetting God* is the initial evil. It is this evil that leads people to indulge in lies and violence and, correlatively, idolatry and pride. Through pride, leaders become tyrants who lead their subjects to death (Isa 14:3–21). Through pride, humans make themselves rivals and usurp God's place, thwarting their own identity by disregarding God's. It is only with the memory of God's covenantal promises that we can perceive the coherence of history and of our lives.

Isaiah asks his readers: *Will you have the patience and trust to believe that in the midst of the chaos of disasters and restorations, the covenant is on its way toward its fulfillment?*

Beneath the surface of the harshest oracles, one glimpses the features of a God whose glory is ultimately to heal, forgive, and gather Israel and all nations into the everlasting banquet at which all tears will be wiped away (cf. Isa 25:6–9).

So, within the procession of events is another history that contains the real stakes that determine our final destiny—the destiny both of individuals and nations. In this second "history" we see revealed the plan of God. Isaiah tells of the healing God *wants* to bestow, *is going* to bestow (Isa 19:22; 57:18, 19) on those who acknowledge their faithlessness, those who agree to leave the heights of pride and walk on the low paths of humility. He speaks of the healing of the people that were injured by adversity, of the heart that remembers the covenant. The plan of salvation advances despite God's judgment of sin.

Both Patrick and the prophet Isaiah had the courage to look deeply into the drama of life—to see through the fog of pain and sorrow, in the midst of contradiction and pain— what mystics call the "innocence of life."

Be Still

〜 *Wisdom to guide you:* "Be submissive when things go wrong in your life. Give God's kindness time and room in you. That's all it asks."

Mechtild of Magdeburg[2]

〜 *Scripture to hold you:* "He brought me out into a spacious place. He rescued me because he delighted in me" (cf. Ps 18:19).

〜 *Thought to sustain you:* The Lord wants to heal me.

Being Led

PLACING YOUR WRITING materials close by, settle down into a state of quiet. Make yourself comfortable, yet remain inwardly alert. Choose a phrase to recite with your breathing: *peace, light, I abandon myself, let go, come....* Nothing has to happen. Just give of yourself through a patient presence.

Become aware of your thoughts. One by one, let them go: the past, the future, the worries about the present. Ambitions and dreams and expectations. Be content with the present, because all eternity is in this present moment.

Say good-bye to your thoughts and feelings, and slip down deeper within yourself. Or go to your safe place, deeper or further than you have ever gone before. Breathe softly and, at every exhalation, allow yourself to rest in the peace before your next inhalation.

As you go deeper and deeper, you will probably encounter new places of resistance. Walk gently around them and let them go, reaching a deeper peace.

In this space, ask yourself: *In this moment, what am I afraid of?* Leave space for these fears to arise. You may want to ask yourself this question several times, allowing periods of silence. As they come to you, write these fears down.

Ask yourself: *What do I regret?* Leave silence as you listen deeply within yourself.

Ask yourself: *What have others told me about myself?* Write down what others have said to you, verbally or nonverbally. Concentrate on those things that have had a greater formative (or deformative) impact on your life.

Ask yourself: *What have I had to do in order to be accepted?* What were the subtle messages that you absorbed in childhood, as an adolescent, in your adult life?

Slip down further, letting go of these fears and demands. Unhook your attention from them, and let them go. In the deepest center of your being, where you are truly yourself, you are more than these expectations and manipulations. In this place where you are truly who you were created to be, you are already loved and you have always been loved.

The gracious waters of an eternal fountain spring up in your true self. Here you are called by your real name. Let yourself feel the coolness of the waters of grace flowing in the hills and valleys of your inner landscape. Let the wind caress your face. Let the beautiful array of colors nourish you. Feel the rain as it gently gives growth. Let the peace of this place penetrate you.

Absorbed in this peace, you may experience that you are not alone; instead, you are in relation to another who gives you to yourself. You may be able to say, "You, Lord, give me to myself now. You guide me to find myself. I am utterly derived from you. I do not exist by myself, but only from you as a perpetual gift that you give to me moment by moment."

Do not force anything. At times you may feel absorbed in peace, at other times lost in shadows or resentment. Little by little you may feel the strength of a hand that guides you in this place. Come back to this place again and again.

This is an exercise of the heart, an opening of the senti-
ments and the thoughts to the gift of oneself. Eventually a
sense of gratitude will emerge. When we feel gratitude with
our whole heart, when we realize we are a gift, then we have
truly entered into reality. The work of making peace with
oneself is moving from illusion to this reality. In the words
of the poet William Blake, "Gratitude is paradise itself."[1]

Standing Taller Than Labels

My friend Gary is a police officer. He is also a dad, the
proud father of five lovely girls. He is a husband, a son, a
Catholic, a Christian, a forty-year-old entering midlife.

As a police officer, he knows the law and how to enforce
compliance with the law. Recently he has found himself
asking questions about things that are less tangible, less
concrete: about his faith and about himself. For the first
time, he finds himself wanting to understand "why" things
are the way they are, daring to express his own opinion. It
is a heady and disconcerting time for him.

One morning, just after the death of John Paul II, AOL
announced, *You've got mail* from Gary:

> The death of the Pope has made me "go back to the begin-
> ning" of my faith somewhat. The Church can appear to be
> a "huge machine" traveling through time, but on that jour-
> ney it has made history, been history, and will be history.
> We are all tied to it, and to Jesus. It has left its fingerprint on
> the world and all peoples forever.
>
> I still wonder about all the people who came before the
> Church, the thousands of years before the Church. I
> wonder how they found God and how they worshiped and
> developed ideas about him. How they incorporated these
> ideas into their daily life. I sometimes wish I could get away
> and become one with the earth, which was created first, in
> an attempt to realign myself.

This thought brought to mind how much we live according to the labels in our lives. I/we seem to construct ourselves according to the labels that are given to us, by ourselves or by others. We then live or act a certain way because it is "expected" of us. I feel like I have spent so much time a certain way, because I was supposed to be that way, that I have lost who I really am. I have so many labels—cop, father, husband, Catholic, Christian, son—and everyone has expectations of how I "should" be. I have no idea what my label for "me" means anymore.

There are times when I feel I haven't measured up to success because my house is not the biggest or the best, measured up to being Catholic because my children don't go to Catholic school or don't completely know the vocabulary of our faith, or measured up to being a husband because I am so busy with things that my relationship with my wife suffers. All of this weighs so heavily on me. All the different personalities in our house seem to be leaning in different directions, as I guess they should be as they grow and develop, and I can't seem to gather them and put them in the direction *I* want. Or, to put it a better way, as I believe they *should* be going.... See, I am doing it myself!

GARY, LIKE SO MANY people today, is wandering. He watches a movie here, hears a comment there, asks a question somewhere else, trying to put it all together. Indeed, today a tremendous amount of information about almost everything is floating around. We have moved quickly from a culture rooted in a Judeo-Christian foundation to a rootless, "democratic" hodgepodge that each person feels a right to navigate alone.

Wandering can be a stage of life: a time of doubting or searching for a deeper understanding of what one has believed "unconsciously" for so long. Wandering can also be a way of life: an eclectic combining of curious and fascinating images and myths, resulting in the creation of one's own belief system.

The Israelites were struck with this wanderlust. The Book of the prophet Hosea likens the Israelites' wandering from the worship of the Lord to the false worship of the gods of their neighbors in terms of a broken relationship that caused great suffering to the Lord.

The beginning of the book offers a startling image: the Lord commands the prophet Hosea to marry a prostitute. The Bible often uses human relationships—especially marriage—to symbolize God's relationship with his people.

God loves his people as a husband loves his bride. And yet, the deepest love of a man and woman is but a shadow of the tremendous love that God has for us. The words "leaping," "bounding," and "gazing," which describe the way God seeks us, and the insistent invitation to his loved one to "arise" and "come away" with him, express the intensity and the passion of this relationship initiated by God.

Yet Hosea was commanded by the Lord to marry the prostitute Gomer, a woman who represented infidelity in a most intimate relationship. The prophet's marriage symbolized the "quarrel" that existed between Israel and the Lord. Israel had abandoned the Lord to worship the idols of the people who lived around them. The Lord considers Israel's worship of other gods prostitution: the breaking of a most intimate relationship, the refusal of an immense privilege. "You are not my people and I am not your God" (Hos 1:9).

In the second chapter of Hosea, however, the Lord's heart overflows with the desire for reconciliation, and again the Lord takes the initiative:

> Therefore, I will now allure her,
>   and bring her into the wilderness,

and speak tenderly to her.
From there I will give her vineyards,
    and make the Valley of Achor a door of hope.
There she shall respond as in the days of her youth,
    as at the time when she came out of the land of Egypt.
    On that day, says the Lord, you will call me, "My husband."... And I will take you for my wife forever; I will take you for my wife in righteousness and in justice, in steadfast love, and in mercy. I will take you for my wife in faithfulness; and you shall know the Lord. (Hos 2:14–20)

The Lord's love is totally gratuitous. Even though he knows Israel will still be unfaithful at times, the Lord wants to bring his people far from the false idols they are worshiping to give them divine gifts. These gifts are justice, tenderness, fidelity, and righteousness.

Israel, however, continued to break God's covenant of love. God states, through the prophet Hosea, "Your fidelity is like the morning dew—it does not last" (cf. Hos 6:4).

In some of the most beautiful verses of the Old Testament, God cries out in pain:

When Israel was a child, I loved him,
    and out of Egypt I called my son.
The more I called them,
    the more they went from me;
they kept sacrificing to the Baals,
    and offering incense to idols.
Yet it was I who taught Ephraim to walk,
    I took them up in my arms;
    but they did not know that I healed them.
I led them with cords of human kindness,
    with bands of love.
I was to them like those
    who lift infants to their cheeks.
I bent down to them and fed them.
They shall return to the land of Egypt,
    and Assyria shall be their king,

because they have refused to return to me.
...How can I give you up, Ephraim?
How can I hand you over, O Israel?
...My heart recoils within me;
    my compassion grows warm and tender.
I will not execute my fierce anger;
    I will not again destroy Ephraim;
for I am God and no mortal,
    the Holy One in your midst,
    and I will not come in wrath. (Hos 11:1–5, 8–9)

Israel had to learn that religion is not about doing or believing the right thing. Religion is about revelation: who God reveals himself to be. In this revelation, and only in this revelation, could Israel truly know herself. When she wandered off to other gods, she no longer knew herself.

Gary is discovering this healing power of revelation. The revelation of God in Jesus is a call to a decision, a call to leave behind our own criteria and to make an act of *faith*.

We believe that God meets us in Jesus. Jesus represents God in the world as the One who bestows Life and reveals the Father. The Church is the mystery of the body of Jesus. It stands wide open, but, unlike other sociological institutions, the Church's depths defy our sounding. This is the revelation God has made to us. We do not need to rely on guesses or insights. We only need to answer, to respond with belief. Belief finds its own equilibrium through ways that are often unseen. Incredibly, it is only in believing that we know who *we* truly are. We can stand taller than labels, peel away criticisms, and go beyond curiosity to adoration.

Be Still

~ *Wisdom to guide you:* "It should be known, then, that God nurtures and caresses the soul, after it has been resolutely converted to his service, like a loving mother who warms her child with the heat of her bosom, nurses it with good milk and tender food, and carries and caresses it in her arms. But as the child grows older, the mother withholds her caresses and hides her tender love; she...sits the child down from her arms, letting it walk on its own feet so that it may put aside the habits of childhood and grow accustomed to greater and more important things."

St. John of the Cross[2]

~ *Scripture to hold you:* "When I was a child, I spoke like a child, I thought like a child, I reasoned like a child; when I became an adult, I put an end to childish ways" (1 Cor 13:11).

~ *Thought to sustain you:* It is only in believing that I'll know who I truly am.

STEP EIGHT

Healing Memories

BY THE TIME YOU REACH this chapter, you will have gathered many memories in the previous exercises, memories
that Jesus wants to heal.

Read through your journal again, and notice what seem
to be recurring attitudes, behaviors, or memories that have
had the greatest influence on your life. In a place of prayer,
alone or with a guide, draw a circle on a blank sheet of
paper. Write these strong or recurring memories inside the
circle. On the outside of the circle, write the feelings that are
provoked by these memories. Draw an even larger circle
that encompasses all of these memories and feelings, and
write around the circle one of the following Scripture
passages:

"Who can separate me from the love of Christ?" (cf.
Rom 8:35)

"If God is for us, who can do anything to hurt us?" (cf.
Rom 8:31)

"Do not be afraid, you are worth more to me than a
whole flock of sparrows" (cf. Mt 10:31).

"Ask and it will be given to you. Knock and it will be
opened to you. I promise" (cf. Mt 7:7).

"Come to me and I will give you rest" (cf. Mt 11:28).

Settle into a quiet space—quiet both within and about you. Ask the Holy Spirit to fill the room where you are. Say the following short phrases slowly, allowing the sense of God's presence to sink deeper and deeper within you.

> Lord Jesus, I thank you for my life.
>
> Lord, I am your child and you know everything about me.
>
> Thank you for loving me so much.
>
> Lord, I ask you by the power of your Holy Spirit to bring to mind the memory you want to heal.

Take one of the memories. It can be from any time in your life, from your life in the womb to yesterday. Go back and reexperience the memory. See yourself as vividly as possible.

After a few moments of silence, invite Jesus, however you may envision him, into that memory. Pray:

> Lord, I thank you for bringing this memory to my mind.
>
> Be with me in this painful, confusing time.
>
> Speak to me and show me what you want me to do.
>
> I ask you to heal this place of hurt.
>
> Come into this memory, Lord, with your love and holy presence.
>
> Come with your healing power.

Pay attention in your imagination to what happens next. Let Jesus appear in your mind's eye.

Imagine Jesus coming to you in that memory, just as you were in the event that has caused so much pain, and with great simplicity watch what Jesus does.

Let Jesus speak to you in your imagination. Let your body experience Jesus' presence.

How does Jesus respond? What does he do? What does he say?

Be patient and let the experience play out.

After a few moments, when you feel a newness within you or a shift in the memory, pray:

Lord Jesus, I thank you for the gift of your life and your love, which has reached into this painful aspect of my life, transforming and renewing me.

Imagine yourself acting, speaking, and thinking now in this newness Jesus has brought about in you. And then pray:

Lord Jesus, if there is anything for me to forgive, I forgive.

If there is anything for which I need to be pardoned, I ask for your mercy.

If there is any reconciliation that is needed between myself and another,

I trust that you will bring about the circumstances in which this may occur.

I turn over to you my life in absolute trust. Amen.

This prayer can be used for the healing of each of the memories that still influences your life. It also could be used more systematically by praying for the healing of each of your stages of life, beginning with your life in the womb.

Sometimes I Feel Like a Motherless Child

"Brother, is it too late to turn around?"

Arlen, a young Capuchin Franciscan, shared with me his recent experience on an immersion trip to Honduras. Five

Capuchins had been sent to deepen the process of being stripped socially and spiritually, preparing them to minister to Hispanics in the United States. They were asked to let go of their language and culture and to experience viscerally poverty, dependence, and weakness so that their ministry would not emerge from power or condescendence, but from mutual understanding and trust: hallmarks of authentic Franciscan poverty.

Brother Arlen laughed as he recounted how many times he asked the question, "Brother, is it too late to turn around?" The last time was as he and his companions arrived at the airport in El Salvador, from which they were going to cross the border into Honduras.

"We arrived in Honduras the next morning," he recounted, "and our experience formally began. Over the next few weeks we experienced the kindness and faith of the local townspeople, the beauty of the mountain ranges, and the feeling that 'We're not in Kansas anymore.' Honduras is one of the poorest countries in one of the poorest parts of the world, and our surroundings gave evidence of that. From the quality of housing and roads to hearing the stories of the townspeople, we knew that we, as North Americans, had blessings that most people around the world can't claim. It was a humbling experience."

Brother Arlen's struggle with low self-esteem quickly made its reappearance. It seemed to him, at least initially, that all the other guys had gifts and talents that were helping them to adjust and make the best of the experience. "I felt I was the only 'dope' in the crowd that was having trouble adjusting. I thought I must be doing something wrong, or that there was something in me making me feel this way. I had a hard time figuring out where God was in all of this.

I felt like the words of one of the old spirituals, 'Sometimes I feel like a motherless child....'"

Arlen began to wonder about his future. If he couldn't deal with four weeks in Honduras, how was he ever going to deal with his future assignments? One day during a group reflection period, Arlen felt he had no other recourse but to turn and reach out to the other Capuchins with him. Talking about his difficult experience made him feel better. He no longer had to hold it all in. The leader of the group, Father Mike, encouraged Arlen to trust in God and not to lose hope; he would experience that God truly was with him in his experience—whether it was one of joy or of sadness.

"From then on I began to experience the immersion program with new eyes. I read the Scriptures and prayed with a revived feeling of hope and trust. I grew in acceptance of who I was and where God had placed me. The feelings of low self-esteem that I experienced were still with me, but the gifts of God that I was experiencing through prayer and my relationships with the other friars were greater than that. To a certain extent I will always carry the cross of low self-esteem, but I will also carry with me what I learned in Honduras, that God created me in his image and likeness and with a purpose. That is what matters."

A SEED IS PLANTED and germinates, a flower buds and blossoms in silence, wrapped in the mystery of life received. No applause, no trumpet blasts, not a single word announces the quiet unfolding of a bud into a gorgeous blossom. Those whose eyes delight in beauty often must bow low to catch a flower's perfumed scent.

Such smallness and wordless silence surround and permeate those who suffer from low self-esteem, people afraid to unfold and blossom in their beauty. Yet such silence is also the moment in which a young girl opened her soul and her body to the seed of the Word of God, planted in history to blossom for eternity—our Savior, God become one of us.

Before the majestic announcement—"You are chosen...the mother of the Son of God...the King of Israel..."—Mary, too, was small and wordless. It is in God's presence that we truly know ourselves. The self is grasped only in front of God.

Mary *feels* herself looked on by the Almighty, covered with the holiness of his presence. She enters into that gaze and sees herself as God sees her. "He has looked with favor on the lowliness of his servant. Surely, from now on all generations will call me blessed" (Lk 2:48). Mary claims her smallness; she delights in being a handmaid and servant. It is not false humility that underlies her attitudes, but the wonder and awe of what she knows.

The Son of God whom she now carries in her womb—ah! what must that coming of God into her womb have been like?—is now poor and humble himself. The Creator of the universe is now a tiny babe, entirely dependent on one he created. In silence, the Word grows beneath her heart. Conceived in Mary through the power of the Holy Spirit, the Word of God has come to take us by the hand and lead us into the glory for which God has destined us. A new epoch for humankind had begun.

Mary, a virgin, was confronted with a baffling mystery—a unique event in the history of the world that would never be repeated: She would conceive a child without a human father, and that child would be God. She did not ask herself if she were strong enough or smart enough or good enough to do what the angel proposed. That would only have led to discouragement. She simply said yes; she allowed God to decide everything, to arrange everything. She asked no questions. She raised no dust. She attracted no attention. She joyfully gave God her consent.

In his Gospel, Luke uses words for Mary's consent that are used nowhere else in the entire New Testament in this same way. Her "be it done to me according to your word" was not just a simple acceptance. Nor was it the same kind of "Let your will be done" that Jesus prayed in the Garden of Gethsemane—a prayer of resignation and surrender. Rather, Luke uses a word in Greek that signifies in Mary a joyous desire to collaborate with what God foresees for her. It is the joy of total abandonment to the good will of God. The entire annunciation narrative is really an invitation to joy: "Rejoice, O favored daughter" (cf. Lk 1:28); "May it be to me as you say!" (cf. Lk 1:38).

To respond with a joyful desire to collaborate with God is to respond with no calculations, no weighing of the options, no taking care of important business first. Mary lays everything before God and gives him the prerogative to lay things out as he sees fit. She boldly abandons herself into the hands of the Father, accepting all the risks, submitting herself to all the eventualities and crises that the future might bring. Thus she enters into the salvation event—a mother in faith and a mother in fact.

Though small, Mary participates in the holiness of God! Though small, Brother Arlen is also raised to the dignity of living God's life, through Jesus Christ and in the Spirit. With Mary, he stands between the poverty of our reality and the splendor of this promise.

Be Still

〜 *Wisdom to guide you:* "Whether a soul is wounded by other wounds of miseries and sins or whether it is healthy, this cautery of love immediately effects a wound of love in the one it touches, and those wounds due to other causes become wounds of love."

St. John of the Cross [1]

〜 *Scripture to hold you:* "Be it done to me as you say!" (cf. Lk 1:38).

〜 *Thought to sustain you:* Don't be afraid to joyfully abandon yourself to my plans for you, says the Lord.

STEP NINE

Retrieving, Replacing, and Letting Go of Losses

IN A HOLY SANCTUARY or quiet spot, alone or with a companion guide, take some moments to focus yourself. By now you may have a favorite short prayer, or you may wish to use one of the following:

Quiet. Peace.
Amen. Letting be.
Still. Letting go.

For a short while, let go of your thoughts, your attempts to understand, plan, or analyze. Immerse yourself in silence.

Two emotions have a major influence on our capacity for relationships and intimacy: love and fear.

Fear of intimacy often comes from childhood experiences in which we had to measure up to be accepted. We are afraid of being judged negatively, so we don't risk letting others get close to or know us. The part of us that is afraid of rejection creates a disguise to keep others from seeing our truth.

Fear comes from a belief that we don't deserve love, often because of something done to us in the past. We project this belief out to the world, and it becomes a self-fulfilling prophecy. We get back exactly what we fear.

Ask the Holy Spirit to bring to mind the negative perceptions of the past and the losses that have resulted from these perceptions that still have a hold on you. It could be the loss of something important, the absence of something wanted but never received, or the pain of being denied or rejected.

List your losses and disappointments on a piece of paper, leaving two or three lines of space between each one. When you have finished your list, go back to each perception or loss and determine if what you have lost

• can be retrieved or even attained for the first time,

• can be replaced with something appropriate for your stage in life, or

• should be acknowledged as a real loss and then released.

For example, through someone's influence you may have lost the belief that you are a good person. That belief can be retrieved. What steps can you take to value yourself as a good person? You may need to let go of years of failed relationships resulting from a negative self-image. You can begin to replace these lost relationships by building new ones–for instance, saying yes when others invite you to join them for a meal. In this way, you can put together a journey of small concrete steps toward new perceptions of yourself, which in turn may pave the way to authentic intimacy.

Reread your ideas several days later and put them together in a short plan of life, a contract with yourself for your future. Offer your plan of life to God, reading it over at a strong moment with God–for example, after receiving Communion, during a retreat or time of Eucharistic adoration, or each morning as you prepare for the day.[1]

The Miracle of Re-Creation

It was early, much earlier than she usually arose. It was still dark, but it wasn't worth going back to sleep. Elizabeth turned on the television. Putting on her housedress, she settled into an easy chair and picked up the remote. She switched channels, then got up for a glass of orange juice. When she resettled herself, something on TV caught her attention. Was it something that she heard, or an image that jogged memories long stuffed into the back closets of her imagination? She took a second look.

"Our Father, who art in heaven.... Deliver us, Lord, from every evil...."

The camera panned a small group of people gathered around an altar. A priest held up a white host and said, "This is the Lamb of God who takes away the sins of the world...."

Tenuous familiarity gave way to a sense of peace as she watched the people receive Communion. Or was it a feeling of at-home-ness? Elizabeth wasn't sure, but she liked what she felt. That night she asked God to wake her up early enough the next morning so she could catch the beginning of the televised Mass. Within a few weeks, watching the Mass on TV had crept into her daily schedule. She even looked forward to it.

One day Elizabeth woke up a half hour before the tele-vised Mass and decided to turn on the television. A group of sisters was saying the Divine Mercy chaplet, followed by the rosary. Elizabeth followed along as the prayers were recited, some of them familiar, some of them new to her. When they finished, she took out the yellow pages, looked up the numbers of the two parishes in her area, and made a phone call. The first number connected to an answering service, so she tried the second. After three rings, a priest picked up the phone and said, "Good morning."

"Good morning," Elizabeth responded, almost shaking at her boldness. She continued, "God has chosen you to come to my house and to bring me Communion. I haven't been to Church in eleven years."

Later that day when the priest came to her house, she told him that after her husband died in 1993, she had shut down emotionally, unable to shed any tears. She had been angry with God for taking her husband from her, and she hadn't been in a church since. But as she told her story, quiet tears started to fall. "They are healing tears," the priest told her, and they continued to heal her throughout the following months whenever she prayed.

Some time later, Elizabeth called her niece and told her she had come back to the sacraments. "It is amazing. Ever since I made my confession and received Communion, I have started remembering things that I had forgotten. I have so many memories to bring to God for healing. At age eighty-two, there are many unhealed memories. But there are joyful memories too."

∼

AMAZING THINGS, BRIDGES. They connect. They inspire. Their vast spans baffle the imagination. Fallen humanity needed such a bridge if it was ever to reach God. The first "no" we said to God, the first refusal of his love and his trust, had separated us. A wedge had been driven into the relationship our first parents had enjoyed with God. Deep fissures of pain created an impassible chasm between humanity and divinity, with distances of sorrow too immense to straddle. Seeing our poverty, knowing our weakness, and pitying our erring hearts, God provided us with a bridge to his heart: the Incarnation of the Word in Jesus of Nazareth. His birth was *our* new creation, our re-creation. The ingenuity of God's creative compassion baffles the imagination and defies explanation. In Jesus of Nazareth, humanity and divinity were wedded together. Now there is no way that God and we can be driven apart. Even sin has lost its power to ultimately disconnect and destroy.

We can participate in this miracle of re-creation to the extent that we believe, to the extent that we allow our attitudes and desires to be transformed into those of the person of Jesus of Nazareth, to the extent that Jesus lives in us now. The road straight to the Father's heart is more than a human bridge could ever be. The moment that the Word of God, eternally begotten of the Father, stepped forth into the human condition, Jesus gave himself to all creatures. Jesus did—and continues to do—more than transport us over the original separation that in a sense broke both divine and human hearts. The Son of God transforms us. We must only believe in the Good News: that we are loved this much. The meaning of the life and message of Jesus is that the reign of God is "close at hand." The whole of God is now available for every person who yearns to receive him. This is why it is called *the* Good News.

The Nativity is far outshone by the Epiphany, the manifestation of Jesus to the Magi, to all of us—what the birth of Christ means. We too are caught up in the glory of this only Son of God becoming man. We do not kneel before his crib as the shepherds did, perhaps playing on our flutes and drums in the silence of the night. Instead we are caught up into his mystery and become living members of his body. We are transformed into God's divine life and flow forth anew from God's divine love. We are each living cells of the body of Christ, caught up in a process that is moving toward the moment of cosmic completion, when Christ will be everything in each of us.

Besides the shepherds and the Magi, however, many others lived in the environs of Bethlehem. Hotel owners had too much business the night of Jesus' birth to afford Mary and Joseph lodging. Others slept through the night, oblivious to the bright star overhead and deaf to the angels' chorus. Perhaps there were curious people who couldn't sleep and who had a sensation that something was different about that night.

The people of Bethlehem mirror the people in our world. Some of us hasten to Jesus with joy. Others of us are unaware of the bright light that shines on our path, oblivious to the angels' jubilant adoration of each of the Lord's footsteps on this earth. Some journey long distances to find faith at great personal expense. Others seem to be sleeping. Yet all of us are the body of Christ, and one by one the Word of God in Jesus of Nazareth manifests his glory to each of us, awakening us to our true dignity and the immense glory that is ours for the taking.

Elizabeth literally "awoke" to this glory as it shone through a televised Mass. As she put herself in the "star's" path each morning that followed, she soaked in the light and glory of the Good News. A phone call, instead of a shepherd's journey, brought her face to face with Jesus in the sacraments. As he manifested his glory, as she fell in love, she herself became a bridge to grace and peace for others in her family.

Be Still

~ *Wisdom to guide you:* "You tell me, dear, that you experience God's infinite goodness so intimately present in your soul that you are scarcely aware of yourself.... This is a great grace.... How blessed are the souls who are so lost in God, for they can truly say...I live now, no longer I, but Jesus Christ lives in me."

St. Jane Frances de Chantal[2]

~ *Scripture to hold you:* "My soul magnifies the Lord...for he has looked with favor on the lowliness of his servant" (Lk 1:47–48).

~ *Thought to sustain you:* I am becoming a bridge of grace and peace for others.

STEP TEN

Proclaiming New Beatitudes

SPEND SOME MOMENTS entering into the presence of God surrounding you and within you. Steep yourself in the mystery of Presence, of the God who *is* now and always. Very slowly read the following, taking it phrase by phrase, digesting each thought completely before going on.

> The secret of peace is at-oneness with what is,
> knowing that things are exactly the way they are
>   supposed to be.
> It is our ego that needs to make things different.
> If we do not feed our ego with our attention,
> then we discover the marvels of the present
>   moment,
> even in the crucible of suffering.

Take some moments of silence, watching your thoughts and the feelings they provoke. Write them down. Confront these thoughts and feelings with the following statements:

We often get angry because we are trying to control others.

Writing a script for ourselves or for others to follow is a setup for disappointment, rage, jealousy, and depression.

The only way to peace is to choose peace—with this moment, in this moment, for this moment.

If we are angry, we can be sure that we do not have the whole story. Our perceptions are limited by our projections and agendas.

When we are unhappy, we have chosen a goal we can't have: getting something another won't or can't give us. Instead, choose peace of mind.

To be happy we may have to let go of having the last word.

Unforgiveness allows us to bolster our ego by blaming others. If we let go of unforgiving thoughts, we are free.

We can always choose to see the world differently.

When we stop judging, healing happens.

We are hurt only by our own thoughts and attitudes.

Everything is perfect just the way it is.

Whatever the problem, love is the answer.

Open your Bible and read Matthew 5:1–10. As you read it, imagine Jesus speaking directly to you. What other beatitudes would he proclaim to you? Finish this sentence: *Blessed are you,* [insert your name], *because you....* Share with Jesus, and another trusted companion, the feelings that have arisen during your prayer.

I AM Enough

When I am looking for some sunshine on an otherwise bleak day, I know just where I can find it: at our switchboard. I stop in and absorb the radiance Karen brings to everything about her job as our operator, watching the kind way she engages the people who enter her office asking for everything from a patient ear to a phone number.

One day I discovered that Karen was looking for a new house. "I've been praying about it for a long time," she told me in her characteristic matter-of-fact way. Her husband's two-year unemployment had placed severe financial constraints on their family. Gradually she had realized that they were going to have to sell their home and move to a smaller house.

"My heart was breaking. How could I leave this home I loved so dearly? How could I give up my gardens where I loved to spend the long summer evenings? I really believed that God had given us this home twenty-five years ago. I became more and more anxious, and got lost in endless 'what if' questions. What if my husband hadn't lost his job? What if we didn't have to sell? What if we didn't have to move? What if we couldn't find a place to go? What if I couldn't get over this disappointment?"

One day, when she was praying about it, she heard the words, "If you are unwilling to let go of this physical house, how will you be able to give up your body when I call you home?"

In an instant she said she saw the struggle we go through, letting go of our earthly dwelling at death when Jesus calls us to a greater, happier place. Then she heard the words within her, "I AM enough."

"In a little way I was given the privilege of trusting in the I AM of God, of finding my dwelling spot not in a physical building but in the heart of God. So I'm really home already, because I am within the walls of I AM.

"For me, I AM is a dwelling place of safety, unbridled love, joy from the Spirit that I can share with others. If I allow I AM to decorate my heart, my new home will be filled with blessings. I've got to trust in that."

THE HURRICANE SEASONS of 2004 and 2005 were particularly catastrophic for the United States, with many people losing their homes. Lives and property had been lost on a scale not seen in recent decades, and certainly the aftermath of Hurricane Katrina was never "expected" in a developed country. The parents of a friend of mine lost their home in Hurricane Ivan.

For twenty-five years the Kerrys had lived on Pensacola Beach, Florida. They had raised their children there, establishing long-lasting friendships. The profound spirituality of New Orleans, which they had brought with them when they moved to Pensacola Beach, had upheld and guided them throughout their life.

Then Ivan came along.

Angela Kerry explains, "When there is a hurricane, the winds begin to tear around the house and sand blows down the street. It always gives me an eerie feeling. Ivan gave me an even stronger sense of dread, since it was heading directly toward Pensacola Beach. I remember, as Ivan was gaining strength, my husband, Joe, said to me, 'We may never be in this house again; let's go down to the corner store and get some steak.' So that's what we did. We had a steak dinner in our house, and then we packed and left. I remember it being so desolate as we drove away."

Angela and Joe traveled inland to their print shop in Gulf Breeze, hoping to weather out the storm there. However, they were evacuated again. They spent a week with Joe's brother before returning to Gulf Breeze.

"We didn't get back to our house on Pensacola Beach for over a month. We had to wait for them to repair a bridge. For all of us it was a long wait.... The worst was not knowing if we had anything left, being in limbo between starting over or picking up where we'd left off."

When the Kerrys finally returned to their house, just about everything they owned was gone. The porch from the house next door had hit their living room extension, opening up a huge gap through which all their furniture and appliances had been sucked out. All the windows on the ocean side had been knocked out.

"My son came with us to check out the house. I think that is when it started to hit us—what we had lost. We'd pick up a piece of something we recognized, and little by little it would dawn on us, 'Oh, that's gone.' We had already given away to our children anything of real value. We found our clothes hanging up and full of sand, and dishes still in the cabinets. But the books and just about everything else was gone. We continued to look for one special statue, however. It was a six-foot Sacred Heart statue my mother had been given by a Good Shepherd sister in Louisiana. The statue had weathered all the previous storms and had become a 'member of the family,' enthroned in a place of honor in all our homes."

The statue must have been shattered by the storm, for the Kerrys found only bits and pieces of it. "Finally, we found one piece large enough to indentify: the heart had not been shattered; it was still in one piece. We were deeply moved. We still have the heart of the statue of Jesus inside a plastic case. As my daughter, who loves Scripture, said, 'It is a sign that "deep waters cannot quench love."' In the midst of the devastation, we still found love."

Angela spoke easily about the loss of her home and how they made the four-room apartment attached to their print shop into their new home. "We lost a lot, but now we live in another beautiful place among the trees, grass, and God's beautiful creatures. We are right behind our son's house; in fact, our backyard and his backyard are connected. It's a small house, but much bigger than people in many other countries have. We have nine beautiful grandchildren, whom we see all the time. We are in good health and love our family so much. We love others, too—the people in church, in the nursing homes we visit—and I imagine our list will increase as we get to know others."

Joe added, "We didn't really lose anything in the hurricane, because we still have everything that is most important to us: our faith, our family, our friends!"

IN THE HEBREW SCRIPTURES, God states that his name is I AM (Ex 3:13–14), and the prophecies of Isaiah illustrate what God means by revealing his name as I AM.

> But now thus says the LORD,
>> he who created you, O Jacob,
>> he who formed you, O Israel:
> Do not fear, for I have redeemed you;
>> I have called you by name, you are mine.
> When you pass through the waters, I will be with you;
>> and through the rivers, they shall not overwhelm you;
> when you walk through fire you shall not be burned,
>> and the flame shall not consume you.
> For I am the LORD your God,
>> the Holy One of Israel, your Savior. (Isa 43:1–3)

I AM is a God of the future, walking, journeying, relating, providing, protecting, transforming, consoling, believing the people he loves. I AM—God—is in relationship with us, always creating and re-creating us. God is always present to what we are experiencing—not distant, aloof, or impotent but close and powerful. We really matter to God because we *belong* to him.

God is concerned about our safety and our future, so much so that God is completely invested, so to speak, in the reality of his people. God delivered the Israelites from Egypt, walked with them through the desert, gave them a land, made of them a nation, and purified them when their hearts were lured by idols and seduced by the wealth of other nations. God was right in their midst, present to the reality of the Israelites, as he took their destiny into his own hands and delivered them again and again from oppression.

And then God did the unthinkable, the unfathomable. It was almost as if God said, "Forget everything that has come before. If you think *that* was great, just wait and see what I will do now!" God became a human being in Jesus, tied even more completely to our destiny, immersed even more truly in our reality.

In the Exodus, I AM had appeared to his people, protecting and guiding a fleeing, frightened people as a pillar of cloud by day and column of fire by night. Later in Jerusalem, each year on the Feast of Tabernacles two great lamps were lighted in the courts of the Temple after sunset—lights so bright that they illuminated the entire city. Jesus stood up before the people and said in words that were an unmistakable reference to the Lord's name: I AM the light. I, Jesus, am the true light that comes into the world. God has taken on a face, and you hear his voice in me because I am God. I am. I AM.

I AM the light of the world (cf. Jn 8:12).

I AM the bread of life (cf. Jn 10:11).

I AM the resurrection and the life (Jn 11:25).

I AM the gate for the sheep (Jn 10:7).

I AM the good shepherd (Jn 10:11).

I AM the resurrection and the life (Jn 11:25).

I AM the way, the truth, and the life (Jn 14:6).

I AM the true vine (Jn 15:1).

The night before he died, Jesus spoke to his disciples no longer as servants, not as a teacher to pupils, but as a Friend to friends. He tried in every way imaginable to make them understand that he was the way to the Father; that was why he had come, that was what he was all about: "If you love me you will keep my words and my Father will love you" (cf. Jn 14:23). Loving the Father and being loved by the Father eventually lead to living in the Father's house. This is the goal of human life.

Karen heard God telling her: I AM enough. I AM here for you. The point is: I AM with you. I AM there, wherever it may be–I am really there. Build your house now in I AM.[1]

Be Still

~ *Wisdom to guide you:* "The only happiness in this life is that of those who have peace of mind in the midst of the troubles of their daily existence; they taste the joy of the children of God.... The good God, the Blessed Virgin, the angels and saints are about our path; they are at our side and see all we do."

St. John Vianney[2]

~ *Scripture to hold you:* "The Lord is my shepherd, I shall not want.... [H]e restores my soul" (Ps 23:1, 3).

~ *Thought to sustain you:* I long to live in my Father's house.

PART THREE

Mystery

The Day

Dawn breaks. Life explodes—
set in motion by a Presence unseen.
Fragile nudity Innocent beauty Pristine novelty
latent with endless possibility.
Thrust forward toward a Future unknown.
Morning Comes. Light unfolds—
Revealing a universe unblemished.
Breathless discovery Captive revery Stunning imagery
latent with endless mystery.
Arousal of inner joy yet unnamed.
Afternoon. Scorching heat—
penetrates all I love and truth unveils.
Harsh reality Listless anxiety Lost serenity
latent with endless complexity
all former pleasures now uninviting.
Twilight falls. Doubt descends—
casting shadows, death and grief unnoticed.
Obscure subtlety Total insecurity Horrid ambiguity
Latent with endless uncertainty.
Haunting disbelief causes acts unwilled.
Night is nigh. Wrapped in dark—
Shrouding senses and soul in peace untold.
Utter solemnity Absolute majesty Coveted integrity
latent with endless eternity.
Union of love with a Presence unseen.

Redefining Power

USE YOUR FAVORITE WAY of entering into prayer and the sacred presence of God. After a few moments of silence, continue.

Our lives can be transfigured and transformed through experiencing Jesus' personal attention. The following is a short guide to this way of praying, which employs the use of memory and imagination:

Choose a situation, past or present, that you wish to bring to Jesus in prayer. Think of a Gospel story that speaks to your situation or the way you feel about it. If you need help thinking of a story, leaf through the books of Matthew, Mark, Luke, or John in the New Testament.

In your imagination, picture the Gospel story as it unfolds. Place yourself in the scene as one of the characters of the story, someone observing or interacting with the others, or simply as yourself.

Begin to speak to Jesus or get involved in the action of the Gospel event. Allow the event to play itself out involving you, even if the "story" continues beyond what is actually written in the Gospel. Notice what Jesus says and does, the way you react and feel, what you say and do.

End when Jesus has finished interacting with you. Finish with a prayer of gratitude and the Our Father.

Not Abandoned, After All

A friend of mine from school stopped me one evening, asking if we could get together just to talk about things. Later that week we found ourselves sitting down to some coffee and a blessedly free evening.

Mary Kate is a very competent, accomplished woman who is profoundly spiritual. I wasn't exactly prepared for what she had to share with me, since it was a part of her life I had known nothing about. "Recently I've begun to work through some issues," she began. "I've been working with a wonderful therapist and spiritual director. It's kind of hard to share, but I'm at the point that I want the people closest to me to know about it. I guess I'm asking for support."

After a bit of silence she continued, "I've been trying to understand the anger and terror that I've carried with me all my life. It's gotten to a point that it's no longer healthy. I had to stop and look at what was going on.

"It all stems from the fact that I was sexually assaulted twice at knifepoint before I was fourteen. This was something I had just taken for granted as part of my life, a part of my life that was over and done with. What I didn't realize is that the intense anger and fear that I feel even now is tied to those experiences. People think I'm bossy and opinionated at work–they probably think I'm full of myself. If only they knew. I'm so frightened inside."

I reached across the table and took her hand. "I'm so sorry," I said softly. I too had sometimes been put off by her snappish remarks and self-assured attitude. How blind I'd been. How self-righteous. Mary Kate was suddenly trans-

formed for me from someone arrogant into someone coura-
geous.

Many adults who suffered trauma in childhood cut themselves off from their child-self in order to cope with daily life.
As children, they shut down emotionally during the traumatic events they experienced to protect themselves from
the horror of what was happening. As they grew into adult-
hood, however, they often remained dissociated from that
part of them that bears these scars—thus keeping both the
experiences and the person who experienced them at a
distance. So I immediately grasped the special grace of what
Mary Kate related to me next.

"I wanted to share with you an experience I had when I
was on a weekend retreat down in Cambridge. I had always
kept a part of myself—myself as a child—in a closet and was
afraid to let her out. I didn't want anything else to happen
to her. I didn't even interact with this 'child' myself; it was
too painful.

"One day, my spiritual director assigned to me the fifth
chapter of Mark: the raising of the daughter of Jairus and
the healing of the woman with a hemorrhage. I read the
passage and began to settle into prayer.

"Well, I certainly could relate to the daughter of Jairus.
Part of me does feel like it has died. The only problem is
that I didn't have a father who was willing to go out of his
way to help me or find someone who could. No sooner had
I thought this than something else crossed my mind, something that I don't think I thought myself: *Maybe that's true of
your own father, but it's not true about me.*

"At that, something began to unfold within my imagination. I saw myself walking hand in hand with my dissociated child-self. Jesus was walking toward us. When he reached
us, although he did not say anything, I knew that he want-

ed me to give my child-self to him. There was something about the way he looked at me; I knew I could trust him. So, I gave her to him. He gathered her into his arms, almost like a mother would gather an infant. The look in his eyes as he gazed at the almost-lifeless form was one of tremendous sorrow and compassion. I could tell he was very sorry because of what had happened to her.

"He turned around and began walking. With a motion of his head, I knew that he wanted me to follow. I did—at a distance. Eventually, he reached a place that was covered with lush, green grass and sat down. I stopped when he sat down and did not continue moving forward. He looked back at me and then looked at the ground next to him, as if signaling me to sit down beside him. I did.

"The next thing I knew, he put his arm around me and gently pulled me toward him. I looked to see where my child-self was; she had disappeared. I panicked and began looking around for her. Jesus pulled me in a little closer. Then I realized that I was that child. Up until now, I had always felt that we were separate. At some level, in this prayer with Jesus I had become integrated, and although there is still a lot of healing that has to take place, the child in me that had died began to come to life again."

I sat in silence, reverencing the sacredness of her story. Our coffee was getting cold as we both absorbed the impact of what she had shared. At last she broke the silence, stating, "I guess my Father had not abandoned me, after all."

~

If there is anything we need today, it is to rehabilitate the image of Jesus' Father. People suffer such violence perpetrated against them. Often they can't reconcile this evil with the existence of a loving God, especially when well-meaning persons tell them: "Well, everyone has their cross to bear." What is that supposed to mean? Does it mean that God planned this cross for me? Does it mean that God is at the bottom of the evil in the world? Does it mean that God is so impotent he couldn't do anything to stop it, so the best we can do is "offer it up"?

Jesus' transfiguration on Mount Tabor indicates how to understand the truth of the events of our lives. The three apostles—Peter, James, and John—look on as Jesus' garments become radiantly bright. Caught up in ecstasy over the event, Peter wants to build a tent and capture this moment for all eternity. How right Peter was! How quick to catch on. He recognized in an instant that this display of Jesus' power and divinity was not some divine fireworks display. Nor was it a frightening display of God's presence, as on the mountain of Horeb before the Israelites who were escaping Egypt. Rather, it was the whole reason for which Jesus had come: to transmit the transforming and life-giving splendor of eternity; to give himself as the Light of the world, selflessly, incessantly, and inexhaustibly.

We are all meant to be immersed in that glory shining forth from Jesus on the mountain. The three disciples who were present were being initiated into the life of the Trinity, the life of divinization to which all are invited.

As the transfiguration scene unfolds, the Father's voice announces the only words attributed to him in the New Testament: "This is my Son, the Beloved; with him I am well pleased; listen to him" (Mt 17:5). The Father points to the Son twice in the Gospels: at the baptism in the Jordan and at the transfiguration. "Listen to Jesus." Our glorification depends upon how well we listen and obey the One who has been glorified, that we too might share in his glory.

Then Peter understood what Jesus meant when he prophesied his own death (Mt 16:21). Jesus meant what he said when he proclaimed, "Take up your cross and follow me" (cf. Mt 16:24). In other words, to share in the glory of Jesus present before them, they must follow his path to Calvary. Clinging to Jesus becomes our new mode of life.

The Father did not instigate the violence by which Jesus died. From the earliest days of our race, our exercise of power has been one of violence: wanting the goods of others, wanting to be ahead, and wanting to be in charge. The last seven of the Ten Commandments all speak to a situation of people fighting among each other:

"You shall not murder."

"You shall not commit adultery."

"You shall not steal."

"You shall not bear false witness against your neighbor."

"You shall not covet your neighbor's house."

"You shall not covet your neighbor's wife, or male or female slave, or ox, or donkey, or anything that belongs to your neighbor." (Ex 20:13–17)

This is in strong contrast with the words of the Beatitudes in which Jesus shows us the proper use of power:

"Blessed are the poor in spirit...."

"Blessed are those who mourn...."

"Blessed are the meek...."

"Blessed are those who hunger and thirst for righteousness...."

"Blessed are the merciful...."

"Blessed are the pure in heart...."

"Blessed are the peacemakers...."

"Blessed are those who are persecuted for righteousness' sake, for theirs is the kingdom of heaven." (Mt 5:3–10)

The Father's power is good and lifegiving. When the world turned its violence on the Father's Son, he did not "put those wretches to a miserable end" (Mt 21:41) as in the parable of the owner of the vineyard. Rather, he strengthened Jesus to endure his torture and persecution without hate or feelings of revenge, but with trust, hope, forgiveness. The Father strengthened Jesus to love his enemies while they hated him. Rejection put Jesus on the cross, but it is precisely on the cross that he fulfilled the Father's need to communicate his love for us and the goodness of his power.

If this is the way God intervened in the suffering of his own Son at the violent hands of another, this is the way God will intervene in the suffering of anyone who trusts in him.

Jesus came to Mary Kate in a visualized prayer, healing her and leaving her more integrated and complete. Though she had passed through years of pain and anger at what had happened, at not being helped by her mother, and at the personality conflicts with which she now lived, Jesus came to her in the power of his glory and the mercy of his own surrender to the violence of others, shaping her a little more in the image of the Father's heart and the Son's obedience.

Be Still

⁓ *Wisdom to guide you:* "Let us then without anxiety suffer the outer shell of our life to humiliate us in our own eyes and those of others, or rather let us hide ourselves under this shell and enjoy God who alone is all our good. Let us make profit of this infirmity...so as to find all our good in the enjoyment of God who by these things gives himself entirely to us as our sole good."

Jean-Pierre de Caussade[1]

〜 *Scripture to hold you:* "See what love the Father has given us, that we should be called children of God; and that is what we are" (1 Jn 3:1).

〜 *Thought to sustain you:* Mold me, Lord, in the gentleness of your love.

Learning Discernment

To MAKE PEACE with ourselves, sometimes we need to make important decisions, and we need God's help to see where wisdom lies. This is called discernment.

When we are learning to discern, it is helpful to follow a method. After centering yourself in silence, letting the "dust" settle, ask Jesus to move your will to choose that which will give the most glory to God for the salvation of the world.

Clearly **state the decision** you need to make. Frame it in the following words: "Option A is..." and "Option B is not doing Option A." (Don't try to list another option—you can only discern one thing at a time, such as, *I do this or I don't do it.*) Write down all the information you have at hand regarding the issue that requires your decision. If you discover you need more information, write down the information you need to get.

Write out your feelings surrounding the whole issue. (For example, I feel upset at having to make the decision so quickly. I am afraid of what my mother is going to say. I feel excited about Option A—like I have a possibility of beginning life over. I don't feel any clarity about this issue at all and doubt I can make it on my own....)

Clarifying the issues. Reflect on these **four criteria** as they pertain to your decision:

> 1. Take yourself the way you are. Respect and accept the others and the situation as they currently are, not as you wish they would be.
>
> 2. Balance thinking, feeling, and doing. Make sure all three are involved in the clarification of the issues.
>
> 3. Keep looking at the entire context.
>
> 4. Ask what unifies, builds up, gives hope, and reconciles.

After clarifying the issues, **again write out your feelings.** Notice if there have been any shifts. If so, what are they?

Picture yourself as if you had decided on Option A. Try it on for fit. Write down what are you feeling inside. Do the same with Option B.

Entrust yourself to the Word of God. Find a passage in the Bible that seems to speak to your situation and read it prayerfully. Ask God to shed light on everything surrounding the decision you need to make.

After praying with the Word of God, **write down the pros and cons** for Option A and Option B. Which option seems to be more for the glory of God?

Return to the passage of Scripture and ask for light on your motivations, desires, needs, proposals, larger community context.

Write out the feelings that were stronger or more insistent.

Picture yourself again in Option A. Do you feel consolation: peace, joy, gentleness, serenity, courage, confidence, growth in faith and love of God, a sense of joy even if the option is painful? Or do you feel anxiety, fears, discouragement, unrest, doubts, darkness, irritation, confusion, a sense of being abandoned by God, alone, isolated? Do the same with Option B. Go back and forth for several days doing this; note your feelings, looking out for signs of blind spots.

Make your decision. God wants us to know his desires and plans for us. The process of discernment is based on the certainty that God will reveal his will to us if we ask.

Becoming a Channel of His Mercy

Every once in a while a certain woman calls me long distance. When I first spoke with her, she had called our convent looking for someone to help her grieve with a sense of faith. We quickly struck up a friendship.

Judy's story is starkly simple in its tragic details. Cheryl, her daughter, had died in an accident caused by another party. Judy had lost her husband to leukemia two years earlier, and the loss of her daughter meant that she was now alone. She was so profoundly saddened that she took to her bed for weeks after the accident.

Our conversations were often punctuated by her cry, "What have they done to my beautiful daughter, my daughter! How could this have happened?" For the first time I heard the intensity of the fourth station of the cross, at which Mary meets her son Jesus carrying the cross. I could not hear Judy's sorrowful words without beginning to cry.

She related to me how one day, while she was drinking a cup of coffee, she became aware of a sense of warmth sweeping over her. The sun seemed to cover her with light. Then, as she explained, "I don't know if it was God or just a thought inside of me, but I heard these words: *Judy, your daughter is with me now. She is happy here. Nothing is going to happen to her anymore. She is safe forever.*" Judy said she was filled with unexplainable peace. As we talked about the experience together, and the feelings it brought her, we realized that it could be a "touchstone" for what God's presence felt like. As she moved ahead with decisions she needed to make, she could ask herself, "What kind of peace am I feeling? Or not feeling? Why?"

Judy wanted help to discover what God wanted her to do. Should she sue, should she honor Cheryl's memory in another way, or should she just walk away from the whole thing? I sent her a guide for discerning the will of God,[1] and over the months we quietly observed how the Spirit was moving her heart as she prayed and considered the different options open to her. We paid close attention to how she felt as she considered each possibility.

～

AFTER HIS OWN death, Jesus understood his friends' need to see beyond the curtain that divides this life from eternity.

> Mary stood weeping outside the tomb. As she wept, she bent over to look into the tomb; and she saw two angels in white, sitting where the body of Jesus had been lying, one at the head and the other at the feet. They said to her, "Woman, why are you weeping?" She said to them, "They have taken away my Lord, and I do not know where they have laid him." When she had said this, she turned around and saw Jesus standing there, but she did not know that it was Jesus. Jesus said to her, "Woman, why are you weeping? Whom are you looking for?" Supposing him to be the gardener, she said to him, "Sir, if you have carried him away, tell me where you have laid him, and I will take him away." Jesus said to her, "Mary!" She turned and said to him in Hebrew, "Rabbouni!" (which means Teacher). (Jn 20:11–16)

Jesus, truly risen from the dead, goes to meet Mary in the garden. He notices her tears and her longing to see him once more. Jesus must have been excited to see her as well, and to have her recognize him at last. He had come to assure her that henceforth there would be no more separation between him, his brothers and sisters, and God. They were no longer simply God's creatures, no longer slaves, but friends—God's children and sharers in the Trinity's love and bliss. Through his glorification they had become flesh-and-blood children of his Father. They were inseparable. He truly could say, "What is mine is yours, and what is yours is mine" (cf. Jn 17:10). Together they were bearers of the message of the new creation.

The apostles, who abandoned Jesus in his hour of deepest human need, were no doubt wary as to where they stood in this new creation. They had nothing really to claim. They couldn't say, "I stood by you to the end; I buried you; I was there." Only one of them had been at Jesus' side when he died. The others had learned about it through hearsay, a report delivered to them as they huddled together in fear.

The amazing thing that they discovered after the resurrection was that God did not judge them, did not "grade" them according to their miserable performance. God simply decided in their favor—a gratuitous, madly loving thing to do. God simply said, "Forget it. Here I send you back Jesus with a message: 'Peace be with you!'" Can you imagine how they must have caught their breath, not daring to believe such undeserved mercy? They, through no merit of their own, were now partakers in the eternal life Jesus had talked about at the Last Supper.

Our human spirit longs to know that we are swept up in the merciful wave of God's goodness, which bestows treasures we could never think to ask for. Yet often we end up plodding along, mistakenly thinking this is all there is, this is the best it gets, this must be preserved at all costs.

In the months that followed Judy's experience of God's peace, she went back and forth in her grief, making, remaking, and un-making choices many times. Eventually, almost with trepidation, I gently offered her another option.

"Judy," I said to her, "you speak as if there are only three choices here: to sue, to honor your daughter's memory in a way that helps others, or to walk away. Each of these decisions has pros and cons. But there is another option we have not considered." There was silence on the other end of the phone. I continued, "That option is to infuse an invisible but real newness into the world by becoming a channel of God's mercy. Mercy doesn't necessarily mean forgiving those who were responsible for your daughter's death, at least not at this moment. It doesn't necessarily mean reconciling with them. Mercy is simply an alternative route to justice."

"So you are saying just to walk away?" she asked.

"No," I responded. "Becoming a channel of mercy does not negate having to choose between the three options we have been speaking of these past months. Choosing to become a channel of mercy doesn't necessarily mean you wouldn't sue. It is a choice about where you are coming from, what is moving you to act, and what you hope to achieve.

"As a channel of mercy, you place yourself before God and ask him to use you in any way he sees fit so that mercy might flow into the world and the justice of God's kingdom be brought about. What that does is provide a pipeline for the invisible but very real power of God's grace to flow into the world. This grace of God can do infinitely more than we could ever imagine. God has something in mind for you to become for the world, in memory of your daughter. Offer yourself to God as this channel of his mercy for the sake of the world."

The concept of being a channel of God's mercy turned out to be a turning point in her discernment. Judy called me a few of weeks later. "I have been praying that God would use me. You wouldn't believe the doors that have opened to me. Sister, I have *found* Cheryl. Each day I go to Mass because I crave the Eucharist. After Communion I feel so close to my daughter I almost see her." She was describing to me the same sense of peace she had experienced weeks after the accident. There was something "true" about this experience of God's presence. "Sister, I need to soak up God. I need to know all about God, because God has my daughter now. My daughter is safe. I need to know about heaven, I need to see God."

Months later, Judy called me unexpectedly. "You encouraged me to pray, 'Lord, in all of this may you be glorified.' I am learning that God actually is the center of everything. I need to glorify him in everything. I don't want this hate in my heart any longer, because it is killing me. I am beginning to see it's over. I need to let go of it. Cheryl is fine right now. I now see that God isn't the one behind the evil that happens in the world. It doesn't make sense to be angry at God. I see now that the most important thing I have is my faith. This is my peace."

Be Still

〜 *Wisdom to guide you:* "Let us...trust in God without limit, aware that if only we endeavor to fulfill his will nothing really evil can befall us, even if we were to live in times a thousandfold more difficult. Is it not appropriate to try to overcome or avoid difficulties? Assuredly, to the extent that it depends upon us alone...but without losing our peace of heart, without grim sadness, and what is worst of all a certain unhappy desperation. Such states of soul not only do not help us resolve the problems, but also make us inept for wise, prudent and quick prevention of difficulties. ...Go forward, but in serenity of spirit.... Then, indeed, crosses will become for us the rungs that lead upward toward resurrection and ultimate happiness in heaven."

St. Maximilian Kolbe[2]

~ *Scripture to hold you:* "For we know that if the earthly tent we live in is destroyed, we have a building from God, a house not made with hands, eternal in the heavens" (2 Cor 5:1).

~ *Thought to sustain you:* I need to see God.

Standing Before the Mystery

THE MYSTERY—OF GOD and of life—can lead us to both awe and terror. The most constructive stance before the mystery is silence. Yet our modern, technologically adept minds seem more at home with analysis, seeking instead to understand, explain, and resolve. Instead, surrendering to God and opening to the mystery are the most practical things we can do.

In a quiet space, alone or with a friend or mentor, devote time specifically to your spirit. You may find it helpful to tune in to your breath, watching your body rise and fall with each inhalation and exhalation. As you breathe in, say *Surrender.* As you breathe out, say *Light.*

Since the mind is made to think, trying to stamp out thoughts and distractions is as hopeless as stamping out a forest fire. This is especially true when we are concerned or upset about a situation. When this happens, our minds will try to convince us that we should not lose a moment's effort in figuring out what to do. An inner tyrant demands that we get about our business. Thoughts bang at the doors of our consciousness, presenting their case for leaving mystery behind and responding to outer demands. If we pay attention, many times the impulse for power, possession, and prestige gives vehemence to these thoughts. They appear to represent good sense, practical thinking, or even God's inspiration—but their very urgency gives them away.

Redirect your mind to pictures that help you reconceptualize the emotional charge of the situation. Try these images:

Light.
Dawn.
Brilliance.
A little bird with a broken wing.
A tiny baby calling out for love.
A little girl or boy asking for help.
A desert expanse.
A cloudless sky.
A starry night.
Light surrounding someone with whom you are having difficulty.

As thoughts and urgent feelings arise, return to the image you have chosen. Stand before the mystery as a statement of your trust in the reliability of the unknown, something that the mind, always grasping for certainty, can never fathom. Choose faith.

This prayer, when repeated over a period of time, actually changes situations in surprising ways, opening them to the refreshing breeze of the Spirit.

Accepting the Present Moment

Randy sat across from me, almost reluctant to share his story. "I need to know if God is somewhere in all of this. I need to figure out where *I* am in all of this." He hesitated.

I encouraged, "God is already at work in the whole story. We simply need to uncover the clues and follow the tracks to discover where he is."

"Steve is our only child," Randy continued, "the absolute joy of his mother. We had so many dreams for him—actually *still* have for him. He's thirty years old now and in medical school. During high school his mother noticed that Steve had many friends, but he had no real girlfriends. My wife came to me several times, worried that Steve might have a homosexual orientation. Every time she brought up the subject, I adamantly rejected it. But we couldn't ignore the fact that our son was very unhappy.

"When he was nineteen years old, in his first year in college, he tried to commit suicide. Finally, Steve broke down in tears and told his mother he thought he was gay. She told him, 'I already know.'"

I asked Randy what it had been like for him when he found out his son was gay. "When I found out, I was furious, outraged. I couldn't believe he could be doing this to us. I couldn't even sit down at the same table with him for dinner. I didn't know what was going on and tried to convince him and his mother that it couldn't be true—but in the end, I was really just trying to convince myself.

"I worried about Steve's salvation. I wanted to find anything, anything at all, that could erase the moment Steve said to me, 'I'm gay.' What had gone wrong? What had we done to deserve this?" Randy stopped again.

"Where was God in all of that?"

"It was hard; it's still hard. I prayed like I had never prayed before. I felt like Abraham, having my son taken from me, my future taken from me, and my future grand-children taken from me. I was angry. I was afraid. I was ashamed.

"Finally a priest listened to my story. He helped me let go of what I wanted, let go of what I may never have, so that we could focus on Steve. The mystery of Steve, of what was happening. I sought the face of God, begging for the life of my son. Somehow I believe that I did touch God's face. I believed that God held in his hands both my heart and Steve's. Just as God didn't look on Steve and see 'gay,' I couldn't replace my son's name with the label 'gay.' I don't understand what has happened to my son. I don't think I ever will. We were able to encourage Steve to speak with a counselor or a priest. He is pursuing his medical degree at this point. What the future holds, I don't know. One thing I do know, however, is that the only way I can keep going is to keep accepting the present moment, asking Jesus just to be with me."

IMAGINE THE CASCADING emotions of Jesus' disciples during that final week of his passion and death.... Hiding from the world, only each other's company for three days.... Imagine how it felt to hear the confusing and conflicting reports of Jesus' appearances and the tales of angels. Finally, their sense of comfort as Jesus appeared among them in a new way, only to have him one day bring them to a mountaintop where he was taken from their sight into the glory of God, where he receives royal power. Jesus' "ascension." Such an unfortunate word! It rings with finality—a door has been closed. Jesus has gone to rest from all his toil, and we must carry on alone as best we can. We too quickly end the story and miss the following passages in the Acts of the Apostles.

> When they had entered the city, they went to the room upstairs where they were staying.... All these were constant-

ly devoting themselves to prayer, together with certain women, including Mary the mother of Jesus, as well as his brothers.... And suddenly from heaven there came a sound like the rush of a violent wind, and it filled the entire house where they were sitting. Divided tongues, as of fire, appeared among them, and a tongue rested on each of them. All of them were filled with the Holy Spirit and began to speak in other languages, as the Spirit gave them ability. (1:13–14; 2:2–4)

Peter and the other apostles left the Upper Room and began to address the quickly gathering crowd.

Those who welcomed [Peter's] message were baptized, and that day about three thousand persons were added. They devoted themselves to the apostles' teaching and fellowship, to the breaking of bread and the prayers. Awe came upon everyone, because many wonders and signs were being done by the apostles. All who believed were together and had all things in common; they would sell their possessions and goods and distribute the proceeds to all, as any had need. Day by day, as they spent much time together in the temple, they broke bread at home and ate their food with glad and generous hearts, praising God and having the goodwill of all the people. And day by day the Lord added to their number those who were being saved. (Acts 2:41–47)

The ascension was the beginning of the end times. We live between that first ascension and the *parousia,* when Jesus will place all things at the Father's feet, that God may be all in all (cf. 1 Cor 15:28).

Now at the Father's side, Jesus is much closer to us, "very near to us," as the Byzantine liturgy of the feast of the Ascension states. What is Jesus doing? "He leads captives"– namely, us–to the new world of his resurrection, and bestows his "gifts," his Spirit, on human beings (cf. Eph 4:7–10). His ascension is a progressive movement, "from beginning to beginning."[1]

The ascension is not, then, a particular historical moment, because Jesus and the human race, since the hour of Jesus' cross and resurrection, are one. The ascension is *still* happening, as men and women, one by one, surrender themselves to the power of the Gospel. The ascension is progressive "until all of us come to maturity, to the measure of the full stature of Christ" (Eph 4:13). The opening prayer of the liturgy for the Ascension describes this progressive vertical movement of history in this way: "You took Christ beyond our sight so that we might seek him in his glory. May we follow where he has led and find our hope in his glory, for he is Lord for ever."[2]

Jean Corbon, in his book *Wellspring of Worship,* asserts that Jesus came forth from heaven as "the only Son; now he returns in the flesh, bringing the Father's adoptive children: 'Look, I and the children whom God has given me' (Heb 2:13). The Father's indescribable joy has taken concrete form and embodiment in the countless faces that mirror the face of his beloved Son."[3]

The Ascension is one of the most consoling feasts of the Church. Just as the Word made flesh entered into the very depths of our contradictions and pain, even unto death; just so we in the Word made flesh are lifted up to the Father and bear his name on our foreheads forever. Jeremy Driscoll, OSB, agrees that "here is a salvation designed to touch and move a very tender and often wounded part of the human heart. Dare we hope that our lives and the lives of those we so much love could have infinite value, that what we do now somehow matters for ever? Could the one I love live forever? Can I hope that death does not destroy and finish our love?"[4]

The Ascension is also one of the most awesome feasts we celebrate. The Word of God became *like* us so as to be *with* us, to be God with us. He became "like his brothers and sisters in every respect" (Heb 2:17), so that we might have a brother and priest who could "sympathize with our weaknesses...tested as we are, yet without sin" (Heb 4:15). Human nature has ascended into God and thus has become the norm of every person's being and the norm of history. Only Jesus can claim a total lordship of history, and he casts his light across all the values of the world.

Like the disciples—who stood in amazement and awe as Jesus was lifted from their sight, and who immediately began to live in absolute obedience to him, praying for the gift of the Spirit—Randy found his peace in the One who knows from the *inside* our contradiction and pain. He discovered there was no other way to live the mystery of our life or to live with others in their mystery than to call down the Spirit, the gift given to us in this interim time between the ascension and the *parousia*.

Be Still

 Wisdom to guide you: "I do not know what will happen to me. I only know one thing for certain: the Lord will never fall short of his promises. Jesus keeps repeating, 'Do not fear. I will make you suffer, but I will also give you strength. I wish your soul to be tried and purified through daily and hidden martyrdom.... Beneath the cross one learns to love, and I do not give this to everyone, but only to those souls who are dearest to me.'"

Padre Pio[5]

 Scripture to hold you: "God in Christ has forgiven you. Therefore be imitators of God, as beloved children, and live in love, as Christ loved us and gave himself up for us, a fragrant offering and sacrifice to God" (Eph 4:32; 5:1).

~ *Thought to sustain you:* I call down the Spirit!

Entrusting Another to God

OFTEN WE CANNOT FIND peace because we worry about someone close to us who is suffering or somehow far from God.

Set aside some time to entrust to the Lord the healing of someone you love. This person may need spiritual, emotional, or physical healing.

Open your Bible and read Luke 8:40–56. In spirit, bow down before Jesus as Jairus does, and tell him about the person who needs his healing touch. Express to him your desires. Give yourself time to share the feelings you have. When you have finished, say to Jesus: "Lord, if you have other plans for this person, I trust you. I let my desires go and pray for the strength and the courage for both of us to follow you wherever you may lead."

Spend time in silence, acknowledging the challenge of what you are experiencing. Or share what is in your heart with a friend or spiritual guide. End the prayer by asking Jesus for a special blessing and placing the person into Jesus' open hands.

The Perfect Healing

It was a warm summer night. My friend Sandra and I had driven out of state to attend the funeral of her friend's mother. As the last of the people at the wake left the funeral home, her friend Monica collapsed. The emotionally draining evening had been the culmination of an emotionally draining relationship. Monica and her mother had never been close, their strained relations becoming more pronounced as Monica married and started her own family.

"Why?" she asked quietly. "Why did my mother have to drink?"

Sandra sat down beside Monica and put her arms around her. "I know, my dear Monica. I know the pain in your heart. I too prayed over and over again for my mother's healing, from the time I was a little girl. I was afraid of her when she was drunk. I was different from the other girls my age because my mother was an alcoholic. I had no cupcakes for class parties, no friends over for sleepovers, no one to see my class plays, and *so* much to hide."

Sandra held Monica, who began to grieve for all that she too had lost. Her greatest sorrow was not being able to share her children's lives with their grandmother. Sandra went on, "When I was a teenager I thought I had prayed enough, and I couldn't understand why there was no healing after so many prayers. I demanded of Jesus to know what was going on. Even though I was only about thirteen years old, I heard clearly within, 'Unless you are able to love your mother in her sickness just as she is, not looking for her healing, you don't really love her. Accept your mom just as she is, alcoholism and all.' My mom never recovered, and she died at a very young age."

Monica reached for a handkerchief. "Sandra, how do you do it? How can you speak so kindly about her? I guess I'm angry—angry at all that couldn't be because of her alcoholism and her refusal to get help or try AA."

"I know. It's hard," Sandra said quietly. "When my mother died, I spent a lot of time alone with her at the funeral home. I questioned why God hadn't brought about healing in her life. Why she had been allowed to suffer so much. Sitting there, I began to realize that, yes, I and my family had suffered, but my mother too had suffered. I don't think she ever wanted to be that way."

Monica quietly looked over at her mother. "She looks so serene there, so at peace."

Sandra quietly continued, "At my mother's death, I felt that she had finally received the healing I so wanted for her. I prayed for her so much after her death, worried about her salvation since she was always in such a drunken state and often wasn't sober enough to go to church. It seemed to me that God was saying that her perfect healing had been brought about in her death, that now she was perfectly healed. And I was able to entrust her into God's hands."

The silence that hung in the room was pregnant with emotion. With a sigh, Monica finally stood and said, "Thank you. I guess more than just my mother needed healing. *Both* of us need healing."

~

JESUS WAS TOTALLY immersed in our humanness, in all things but sin. He entrusted himself wholly to the life and to the death that we each experience. He lived the fear and the challenge that open up the horizons of the ultimate reliability of life and death. In contrast to ours, his was a complete acceptance of the eternal now, radiant in each passing moment of time.

The resurrection is the most splendid moment for Jesus *and us.* It ultimately verifies everything he preached to his disciples, all the healings that were wrought by his hand. Because of his resurrection, we have absolute assurance that total healing will be brought about in *our* resurrections—resurrections that happen daily, climactic resurrections that mark transitions in our life, and finally in the resurrection after our death. It has been said, "Resurrection is the most unnoticed and under-appreciated miracle that takes place in common lives."[1]

That is the way it was with Jesus, who rose from the dead before dawn while Jerusalem slept. He slipped into his disciples' lives largely unnoticed by anyone except those who loved him. Our resurrections are often the same. After the tumult and chaos of the "deaths" we undergo, our resurrection healings are often quiet, noticed by those who have the eyes to see us in new ways, and whose seeing frees us.

In his Letter to the Romans, Paul wrote:

> I consider that the sufferings of this present time are not worth comparing with the glory about to be revealed to us. For the creation waits with eager longing for the revealing of the children of God...in hope that the creation itself will be set free from its bondage to decay and will obtain the freedom of the glory of the children of God. We know that the whole creation has been groaning in labor pains until now; and not only the creation, but also we ourselves, who have the first fruits of the Spirit, groan inwardly while we wait for adoption, the redemption of our bodies. (8:18–19, 21–23)

Paul says that the very same Spirit who raised Jesus from the dead is the Spirit who raises us from the dead. It is a guarantee! The sufferings that are the lot of all earthly existence cannot prevent the coming of the promised glory! While we groan on earth, we already have the "first fruits" of the Spirit. We are already co-heirs with Jesus; we have died and risen with him in Baptism through the Spirit. The Father has succeeded in what he had set out to do. He has given himself to us through Jesus in the Spirit—and nothing can prevent him now from glorifying us and embracing us in the intimate love that exists in the Godhead. Nothing.

"[T]he Spirit helps us in our weakness...that very Spirit intercedes with sighs too deep for words" (Rom 8:26). God himself is praying *within* the person in need of healing. God himself is praying *for* the person in need of healing. When he or she does not know what to say to God—even when he or she cannot pray or can only reject the One who has "failed" to magically fix the problem—the Spirit goes on breathing within the person, with groans and sighs that God understands, "because the Spirit intercedes...according to the will of God" (Rom 8:27). When we pray we never do so "on our own." The Spirit is praying in us and for us. We often think of God as listening to "our" prayer, but in reality it is the intercessory power of the Spirit of God that *is* our prayer.

Signs of hope are everywhere. They may not show up in our medical records or financial reports. They lie instead in the absolute guarantee that nothing can remove us from the security of the God who has died to love us. This is the God Jesus entrusted himself to as he hung upon the cross—his ultimate parable, his ultimate wisdom. In the face of death itself, we can entrust ourselves to this God who spends all his heart on finding ways to love us. A modern mystic, Adrienne von Speyr, wrote, "Because once and for all there is hope.... The signs of living hope are to be found every-

where...this hope...that is irresistible.... God leaves no creature without it."[2]

Monica asked, *Why do we not see this hope now? Why do we
go through times of suffering and pain?* Because the ultimate
adoration a creature can make is in entrusting oneself to
God, in waiting on God's time, so that the time of sighing
and suffering may be lifted in the most delicate of resurrection healings. As Von Speyr succinctly puts it, "And the hour
belongs to God." Are God's ways understandable? Often,
no. Are God's ways reliable? After the death and resurrection of the Christ, we can only answer with a resounding *yes!*

Be Still

〜 *Wisdom to guide you:* "From misery to misery we go
from mercy to mercy.... If you are willing to endure in
peace the trial of not pleasing yourself, you will
provide a sweet refuge to the Divine Master. It is true
that you will suffer, since you will thus be dispos-
sessed, but do not fear: the poorer you are, the more
Jesus will love you."

St. Thérèse of Lisieux[3]

〜 *Scripture to hold you:* "Do not worry about
anything, but in everything by prayer and supplica-
tion with thanksgiving, let your requests be made
known to God. And the peace of God...will guard
your hearts and your minds in Christ Jesus" (Phil
4:6–7).

〜 *Thought to sustain you:* The hour belongs to God.

Making a List of New Memories

TAKE WITH YOU THE NOTEBOOK in which you have written your thoughts and feelings as you worked through the steps in this book and go to a comfortable place where you can be alone for about an hour. Perhaps put on some quiet music. Leaf through the pages, reliving your journey into peace. Highlight moments of grace, moments when you felt God's presence in a special way. Make a list of these moments on a fresh page of your notebook. On another page, list the feelings that accompanied such moments of grace.

This is your new beginning. This is a list of your new memories, memories that need to be cultivated, cherished, and reverenced. These feelings are signs and reminders of the presence of God. When feelings of disruption, fear, anger, and depression pull you back into old situations, relationships, and choices, reread this checklist of grace so that your footsteps may remain on the new path of life.

Finally, offer a prayer of gratitude. You might want to choose from the following suggestions:

Write your own Magnificat of praise modeled after Mary's Magnificat (cf. Lk 1:46–55).

Meditate imaginatively with Zacchaeus (Lk 19:1–10) or Mary at the tomb on the morning of the resurrection (Jn 20:11–16).

Revisit a prayer suggestion in one of the earlier chapters of this book that was especially meaningful to you.

Write an autobiography with the theme of light or peace.

This Is Just the Beginning

In Portland, Oregon, I met Del, who was soon to be ordained a deacon. As we sat down to lunch together, he shared with me the story of how he had almost lost his wife, Debbie. On February 10, 1995, a Friday, he had come home from work to find his wife and the dogs gone. Figuring that she had gone out to run the dogs, he sat down to watch TV. As hours went by, he began to prepare supper, only to be interrupted by a telephone call that would change his life forever.

The man on the phone said, "I have bad news. Your wife has been taken by life flight to Emmanuel Hospital. She was run over by an eleven-year-old on a motorcycle."

Del said, "I was stunned. I jumped in the car and drove into town to the hospital. I was thinking, *What has happened? I don't understand what has happened.* When I got to the hospital ER, I was taken into Debbie's room. I couldn't even recognize my wife."

As Del entered the waiting room, he met the father of the boy who had run over his wife. "I'm sorry for what happened to your wife," the man said, "but the motorcycle wasn't mine or my son's. It belonged to another boy. I didn't give my son permission to ride it, so if you're going to sue anyone, sue the owner of the motorcycle." Then he turned around and left. That was the last time Del saw him.

An immediate surgery on the blood clot on the right side of his wife's brain did not go well. After three more hours of surgery, a large vessel in her brain started hemorrhaging profusely. The neurosurgeon told Del there was a good chance his wife would die or suffer serious brain damage. At least the news from the orthopedic surgeon, who operated to repair her left elbow, was good.

Del closed his eyes as he remembered that first night. "I went home but couldn't sleep. I was in total shock. How and why did this happen? I started praying to God like I had never prayed before. The next morning I went to see Debbie. I said to myself, *This cannot be my wife*. Her face was black and blue. She was on a ventilator and in a drug-induced coma to keep her body calm and give her brain time to heal. The neurosurgeon again tried to prepare me for the worst. I stayed with Debbie all that day.

"The next night and the following nights I prayed myself to sleep. I would wake up every twenty minutes and pray some more before drifting off. I had a lot of time to reflect on my relationship with my wife, my relationship with God, and my life's priorities. I realized how much I loved my wife, how empty my life would be without her, and that I might never hold her in my arms again. I had never really thought of my wife as God's gift to me before. In those dark hours, however, I began to see things in a new light. Prior to the accident, my wife had been a conservative Baptist. Many times after she had gone to her Sunday service, she would drag me kicking and screaming to St. Henry's Church for Mass. Usually, however, I had more important things to do than to go to church."

Del continued, "On one of those sleepless nights, I entered into the deepest relationship with God I'd ever experienced. I prayed for God to please give my wife back to me as she was before the accident. But, *regardless of the outcome,* I said, 'God, I'm returning to the sacraments. I'm coming home. No deals!'"

On Friday morning at about 2:00 AM, Debbie came out of her coma and began a slow but complete recovery. After one week in ICU and several more weeks in the trauma ward, she was transferred to a rehabilitation unit at another hospital for four more weeks of intense rehab therapy. In the first week she progressed from a walker to a four-legged cane. The following Friday she was released from rehab and allowed to go home. Her recovery had been almost miraculous! The neurologist stated that Debbie was functioning at a higher level than most people, and that he had not seen someone come back that quickly and that completely in a very, very long time.

As soon as Debbie was able to go out, she and Del started attending Sunday Eucharist at St. Henry's Church, and then they would go to her evangelical church. Del shared with his wife his promise to God that he would "come home."

Del told me, "When I first went to the sacrament of Reconciliation (after over twenty years of not practicing my faith), it was such a relief to hear the words of absolution. It was like a great burden was lifted off my back. It was just—wow!—I can't explain how wonderful it was just to come home. Debbie and I attended classes on the catechism. My eyes were opened to so many things I had never really known before. Then my wife decided to go through RCIA [Right of Christian Initiation for Adults]. One weekend, as we recited the Creed side by side at Mass, I heard her say the words she had always skipped: 'We believe in one holy catholic and apostolic Church.' I knew then that she believed. I went through RCIA with her and learned so much more about my faith."

Del became a eucharistic minister and volunteered with trauma intervention programs. He used his own experience of Debbie's trauma to assist families in traumatic situations. Often he'd be called out two or three times during a twelve-hour evening shift, but he began to love doing ministry work.

Del ended his story with this reflection: "The one thing that I learned is that God is real and does answer our prayers, but not always in the way we want them answered. Often we may never understand why God allows things to occur. My wife's accident brought me back to the Church. I got back everything that I thought I was going to lose, and my eyes were opened to what is truly valuable in life.

"My wife and I have grown so much closer. I volunteer as a Catholic eucharistic minister at two of the local hospitals and was an RCIA sponsor. Just prior to Easter 1999, while on a weekend RCIA retreat led by a priest who had been a Presbyterian minister, in the quiet of my heart I felt the call to deeper ministerial service, a calling to the permanent diaconate. At first I suppressed the idea, but the more I've opened up and let God be active in my life, the more I've felt called.

"We don't always hear God calling us because we allow other things—job, money, sports, hobbies, etc.—to become a priority in our lives. But God is calling us all the time. Often it's only when we are powerless and about to lose everything important that we are ready to hear God speak. God has been very good to me. My wife made a complete recovery, she became a Catholic, and now, with her Baptist background, she is an important part of our parish RCIA team."

Del was ordained a permanent deacon on November 5, 2005, ten years after his wife's accident. "If someone had told me in 1995 that I was going to be ordained a deacon, I'd have said, 'You're nuts!' Now I spend almost ten hours on the weekends doing ministerial service. I see Jesus so much in everything and everyone I talk to. It's a change in lifestyle. A realization of where the real treasures are. But the story has just started. This is just the beginning."

DEL TOLD ME that this experience was a true revelation for him. This walk in the darkness of the unknown and of fear for his wife's life revealed to him just who he was and who he was not. It revealed to him this woman who was his wife, and the love they shared. Finally, it revealed to him the face of God. The woman who had dragged him to church each Sunday had also dragged him to God through tragic paths neither spouse could have anticipated. And he understood the silent appeal of her wounded body. "It is time to come home," he told God. And he meant it.

Their lives had been violently and cruelly thrown to the winds of tragedy; she hung in the balance between life and death, and so did he. The early Christians, for whom the Book of Revelation was written, also lived in a tragic time. They had set out to follow Jesus on the word of the Apostle John, who had been an eyewitness of Jesus' life, death, resurrection, and ascension. Jesus himself they had never seen with their own eyes—and then they found themselves oppressed, imprisoned, and threatened with death because of Jesus' name. They felt their powerlessness; they were tempted to compromise, to assimilate themselves into the culture, to give in and throw some incense on the altar dedicated to the Roman emperor just to save their lives. Their questions were probably the same as Del's: "Why me?" and "How long will you hide your face from me?" (Ps 13:1).

The Book of Revelation recounts the visions of the Apostle John, visions that were meant to console the Christians suffering oppression and persecution. Surprisingly, the book opens not with a condemnation of their persecutors, but by pointing out the sins of the Christians themselves. Each of the churches, except the church of Philadelphia, had been negligent in some way and was called to repentance. And to each of the churches was given a promise:

> To everyone who conquers, I will give permission to eat from the tree of life that is in the paradise of God.... Whoever conquers will not be harmed by the second death.... To everyone who conquers I will give some of the hidden manna, and I will give a white stone, and on the white stone is written a new name that no one knows except the one who receives it.... To everyone who conquers and continues to do my works to the end, I will give authority over the nations.... If you conquer, you will be clothed...in white robes, and I will not blot your name out of the book of life; I will confess your name before my Father and before his angels.... (Rev 2:7, 11, 17, 26, 3:5)

The Book of Revelation seems to tell us we do not have the luxury of sitting in judgment on others. The author of Revelation leaves no place for such time wasting. Only the Lamb of God is able to judge. Only the Lamb is worthy to divide the sheep from the goats, because he—and no one else—has paid their ransom. The rest of us must look to ourselves beneath the power of the piercing two-edged sword that heals even as it wounds.

John gives us a vision of heaven, a collage of scenes in which God is enthroned at the center and everything and everyone else bows in worship. The Lamb who was slain, Jesus, is victorious over all the earth, and in this kingdom there are no more tears or fears.

A shaft of light falls upon us from the throne of God, and everything is revealed. The dust, the dirt, the disrepute. Nothing is spared from exposure to the light, which falls through the crack of eternity's door. Gradually, we let more and more of our lives be washed in this river of light until we are completely and entirely ready to serve and worship God for all eternity. Then we are surprised by the generosity of this God who invites us into the dance of life and love in the Godhead, who pours himself out to hold, to heal, and to hallow all that he has made, and who wishes to live among us.

The Book of Genesis begins with the creation of heaven and earth (Gen 1:1ff.). The Book of Revelation ends with the creation of a new heaven and a new earth (Rev 21:3ff.). Once again, as in the Garden of Eden, as in the stable of Bethlehem, as in the descent of the Spirit at Pentecost, God makes his home among mortals, dwelling with them. "They will be his peoples, and God himself will be with them; he will wipe every tear from their eyes. Death will be no more; mourning and crying and pain will be no more, for the first things have passed away" (Rev 21:3–4).

Be Still

∽ *Wisdom to guide you:* "Believe firmly that there is no worse calamity than losing the friendship of one's God. The more you mount toward him, the more you detach yourself from the earth and its vanities. Be consoled by the certitude of my love. I am in you, and your sorrow loses itself in me."

Jesus to Marguerite[1]

~ *Scripture to hold you:* "Come to me, all you that are weary and are carrying heavy burdens, and I will give you rest" (Mt 11:28).

~ *Thought to sustain you:* God makes his home among mortals. God dwells with me.

Promise Revisited

THIS CONCLUSION IS NOT a short wrap-up to the previous fifteen chapters. Rather, it is a climax—a look at what *God* does so that we might make peace with ourselves. God's love is an event: something that happens, that reveals itself to us *in* the happening. We can know God's love most clearly in the event of Jesus Christ—his life, death, resurrection, and ascension. We can know God's love in the day-to-day revelations of his love—playing itself out in ways that baffle us and turn our ideas of God inside out.

A friend shared with me how worried she was about Rachel, a woman she had known for many years. They had grown up together, gone to school together, and remained friends as young adults, but had drifted apart as each ultimately chose different paths in reference to God. Now Rachel lay dying of inoperable cancer in another state. My friend was worried about her, since Rachel had stopped practicing any religion and expressed almost a hatred for God. Rachel had made it clear that she did not want to see a priest and had refused the last rites.

I led my friend in a prayer of inner healing for Rachel. We closed our eyes and took Jesus to her bedside. We asked

Jesus to heal each stage of Rachel's life, and in particular to heal whatever could have led her to reject God in this way. At the end, I asked my friend what Jesus was doing. She responded quietly, "Jesus is leaning over Rachel and giving her a blessing."

A week later I asked her how Rachel was doing. "Some interesting things are going on," my friend replied. "Rachel has started talking about a picnic that she is supposed to be going to. She says her grandfather and her sister, both of whom passed away years ago, are setting up the picnic. She even knows what she is going to be eating. She's going to have a large glass of ice-cold Coke. But she keeps on saying that something is holding her back from going to the picnic, and she doesn't know what it is. She still won't allow a priest to visit her."

In my heart I knew immediately that this "picnic" was not just a fanciful imagination. We were on holy ground, and I wanted to bow down in adoration of a God who could so creatively pursue Rachel.

My friend continued, "The hospice nurses say they don't understand why she is still alive. She hardly has blood pressure. Her organs are shutting down. She just keeps talking about this picnic she is supposed to go to."

God was not going to let Rachel die without trying every possible avenue to her heart.

"Look, I know her family won't let you go to see her," I told my friend, "but if you can get someone to put a phone to her ear, lead Rachel in an act of perfect contrition. Don't use the formal prayer, but lead her in an act of sorrow in the context of her picnic."

My friend called Rachel. Rachel was sleeping, but my friend got her mother to put the phone to Rachel's ear. "Rachel," she said softly, "I know you want to go to this picnic that everybody in heaven is preparing for you. Now it's time to go, but first tell God that you are sorry for anything in your life that you may have done that was wrong: 'O God, I am sorry for my sins with all my heart. I love you. I want to come to you. I trust you. Amen.'"

Rachel died a few days after. At the funeral, Rachel's brother took my friend's hand and thanked her, saying, "I want you to know that Rachel made peace with God before she died. I know that you wanted that, and I wanted to tell you that it's okay now. She was at peace when she died."

∼

IN HER BOOK, *Confession,* Adrienne von Speyr writes that we who have been absolved "cease for a moment to be what we were; a connection is torn asunder, a world is left behind us and our souls are freed, for a moment at least, for the ascent to God.... We are free with a freedom whose source is the ascending Son, a freedom toward God, better discipleship, becoming a new person."[1]

Confession has a rending power, "so near and real that they need only to reach for it in order for it to transport them up into heaven."[2] Confession also has healing power, a uniting power, a power for reconciling us to God, to the Church, and to ourselves. This power puts us in touch with who we most deeply are; it brings us, and the world, true peace.

Everything in this book up to this point has been a preparation for the peace God brings about when we finally recognize the startlingly radiant gift of his life in our souls. When we who live so much of our lives in semi-darkness catch sight of the radiance of God's life, we do a spiritual "double-take." It is this light that grabs our attention and makes us see another option for dealing with the contradictions, sorrows, and pains of life. The other option is *utter and complete self-abandonment to God, to the point that we* see *the deepest reality at work in the world and in our lives.*

I hope that this line, extracted from the promise at the beginning of the book, means more to you now than when you first started reading. I hope that the act of abandoning yourself to God is more attractive, more trustworthy, more reliable than it seemed before you first picked up this book. We truly can give ourselves to this God at work *within* us and *for* us with complete assurance that our best interests are *always* at heart.

Notes

PART ONE: LOVE

Step One: Settling Down

1. "You Belong to My Heart," English lyrics by Ray Gilbert, original words and music by Agustin Lara, © 1943 by Peer International Corporation and as designated. Copyright renewed. International Copyright Secured. Used by permission. All rights reserved.

2. Susan Saint Sing, *Living with Sickness, a Struggle Toward Meaning* (Cincinnati: St. Anthony Messenger, 1987), 83.

Step Two: Accepting the Past

1. Infant sacrifice was widely practiced in Canaan and in the Phoenician colonies of North Africa. It was not uncommon in the ancient world for parents to sacrifice a son in times of great need or illness, to try to appease the gods. Enlightenment humanism has reduced God's command to Abraham to kill his son to an extrinsic moral demand: When what seems to be God's voice

commands one to go against the moral law, it must be counted as a deception. However, this misses the point of the story. The story shows how Yahweh forbade any human sacrifice, though he accepted the offering of animals. He did not want human flesh; what he wanted most was human faith and trust.

2. Jean-Pierre de Caussade, *Self-Abandonment to Divine Providence* (Rockford: Tan Books and Publishers, 1959), 174.

Step Three: Risking Trust

1. Abraham J. Malherbe and Everett Ferguson, *Gregory of Nyssa: The Life of Moses* (New York: Paulist Press, 1978), 116.

2. Jean Danielou, *From Glory to Glory* (New York: Scribner and Sons, 1961), 57–58; in this respect, Danielou states that sin is ultimately a refusal to grow. See page 60.

3. Thérèse of Lisieux, *Thoughts of Saint Thérèse the Little Flower of Jesus* (Rockford: Tan Books and Publishers, 1988), 96.

Step Four: Exploring Inner Prisons

1. Augustin-Michel Lemonnier, *Light Over the Scaffold* (New York: Alba House, 1996), 27.

2. Ibid., 94.

3. Ibid., 96.

4. Claude de la Colombiere, as quoted in Jean du Coeur de Jésus d'Elbée, *I Believe in Love* (Chicago: Franciscan Herald Press, 1974), 33.

Step Five: Discovering Compassion

1. Thérèse of Lisieux, *Thoughts of Saint Thérèse the Little Flower of Jesus,* 59.

PART TWO: HEALING

Step Six: Choosing Directions

1. For this section, I am grateful to Marco Guzzi for ideas in his book *Darsi Pace* (Milano: PAOLINE Editoriale Libri, 2004), 83–91.

2. Mechtild of Magdeburg, as quoted in Carmen Acevedo Butcher, *Incandescence* (Brewster: Paraclete Press, 2005), 139.

Step Seven: Being Led

1. Guzzi, *Darsi Pace*, 95–97.

2. John of the Cross, *Search for Nothing* (New York: Crossroads, 1982), 133.

Step Eight: Healing Memories

1. John of the Cross, *Search for Nothing*, 138.

Step Nine: Retrieving, Replacing, and Letting Go of Losses

1. I am grateful to Sr. Helen Cote, PM, of the Marie Joseph Spiritual Center, Bidderford, Maine, for sharing with me the process of healing from losses.

2. Jane Frances de Chantal, as quoted by Joann Wolski Coinn, ed., *Women's Spirituality: Resources for Development* (New York: Paulist Press, 1996), 323.

Step Ten: Proclaiming New Beatitudes

1. I am grateful to Sr. Raymond Marie Gerard, FSP, for sharing with me her research and personal reflection on the *Ego Eimi* statements of the Fourth Gospel.

2. John Vianney, as quoted by Alfred Monnin, *The Curé of Ars* (St. Louis: Herder, 1927), 205, 215.

PART THREE: MYSTERY

Step Eleven: Redefining Power

1. Jean-Pierre de Caussade, *Self-Abandonment to Divine Providence* (Rockford: Tan Books and Publishers, 1959), 77.

Step Twelve: Learning Discernment

1. This guide for discernment appears at the beginning of this chapter.

2. Maximilian Kolbe, as quoted by Jerzy M. Domanski, *Maria Was His Middle Name: Day by Day with Bl. Maximilian Kolbe* (Altaden, Benzinger Sisters Publishers, 1977), 133.

Step Thirteen: Standing Before the Mystery

1. The expression is used by Gregory of Nyssa in his eighth *Homily on the Song of Songs* (PG 44:941c). The entire spiritual life is carried along by this "ascensional" thrust.

2. *Vatican II Sunday Missal* (Boston: Pauline Books & Media, 2001), 518.

3. Jean Corbon, *The Wellspring of Worship* (San Francisco: Ignatius Press, 2005), 66.

4. Jeremy Driscoll, OSB, *Theology at the Eucharistic Table* (Rome: Centro Studi S. Anselms, 2003), 180.

5. Padre Pio, as quoted by Gianluigi Pasquale, ed., *Secrets of a Soul, Padre Pio's Letters* (Boston: Pauline Books & Media, 2003), 47.

Step Fourteen: Entrusting Another to God

1. Richard J. Foster, *The Renovare Spiritual Formation Bible* (San Francisco: HarperCollins, 2005), 2056.

2. Adrienne von Speyr, *The Victory of Love* (San Francisco: Ignatius Press, 1990), 64–66.

3. Thérèse of Lisieux, as quoted in Jean du Coeur de Jésus d'Elbée, *I Believe in Love* (Chicago: Franciscan Herald Press, 1974), 39.

Step Fifteen: Making a List of New Memories

1. Jesus to Marguerite, as quoted by the Legion of Little Souls of the Merciful Heart of Jesus, *Message of Merciful Love to Little Souls* (San Rafael: POPE Publications, 1986), 331.

The Promise Revisited

1. Adrienne von Speyr, *Confession* (San Francisco: Ignatius Press, 1985), 112.

2. Ibid., 114.

Bibliography

Hermes, Kathryn. *Prayers for Surviving Depression*. Boston: Pauline Books & Media, 2005.

——. *Surviving Depression: A Catholic Approach*. Boston: Pauline Books & Media, 2004.

Hillesum, Etty. *An Interrupted Life*. New York: Simon & Schuster, 1981.

Keating, Thomas. *Intimacy with God*. New York: Crossroad, 1995.

Klug, Lyn, ed. *A Forgiving Heart: Prayers for Blessing and Reconciliation*. Minneapolis: Augsburg Press, 2003.

Llewelyn, Robert. *All Shall Be Well*. New York: Paulist Press, 1982.

McNamara, William. *Christian Mysticism: The Art of the Inner Way*. New York: Continuum, 1981.

Oberg, Delroy. *Given to God: Daily Readings with Evelyn Underhill*. London: Dartman Long & Todd, 1992.

Wicks, Robert J. *Touching the Holy*. Notre Dame: Sorin Books, 2007.

Williams, Rowan. *Where God Happens*. Boston: New Seeds, 2005.

Wolff, Pierre. *Discernment: The Art of Choosing Well*. Indianapolis, Missouri: Triumph Books, 1993.

BOOKS & MEDIA

The Daughters of St. Paul operate book and media centers at the following addresses. Visit, call or write the one nearest you today, or find us on the World Wide Web, www.pauline.org

CALIFORNIA

3908 Sepulveda Blvd, Culver City, CA 90230	310-397-8676
2460 Broadway Street, Redwood City, CA 94063	650-369-4230
5945 Balboa Avenue, San Diego, CA 92111	858-565-9181

FLORIDA

145 S.W. 107th Avenue, Miami, FL 33174	305-559-6715

HAWAII

1143 Bishop Street, Honolulu, HI 96813	808-521-2731
Neighbor Islands call:	866-521-2731

ILLINOIS

172 North Michigan Avenue, Chicago, IL 60601	312-346-4228

LOUISIANA

4403 Veterans Memorial Blvd, Metairie, LA 70006	504-887-7631

MASSACHUSETTS

885 Providence Hwy, Dedham, MA 02026	781-326-5385

MISSOURI

9804 Watson Road, St. Louis, MO 63126	314-965-3512

NEW JERSEY

561 U.S. Route 1, Wick Plaza, Edison, NJ 08817	732-572-1200

NEW YORK

150 East 52nd Street, New York, NY 10022	212-754-1110

PENNSYLVANIA

9171-A Roosevelt Blvd, Philadelphia, PA 19114	215-676-9494

SOUTH CAROLINA

243 King Street, Charleston, SC 29401	843-577-0175

TENNESSEE

4811 Poplar Avenue, Memphis, TN 38117	901-761-2987

TEXAS

114 Main Plaza, San Antonio, TX 78205	210-224-8101

VIRGINIA

1025 King Street, Alexandria, VA 22314	703-549-3806

CANADA

3022 Dufferin Street, Toronto, ON M6B 3T5	416-781-9131

¡También somos su fuente para libros,
videos y música en español!